20TH CENTURY MUSIC

1900-20 NEW HORIZONS

Malcolm Hayes

CONTENTS

RUSSIANS IN REVOLT
In February 1917, the Tsar of Russia and the imperial government were overthrown by a popular revolution. In October, Lenin (on the steps, with cap and beard) and his Communist Bolshevik Party seized power.

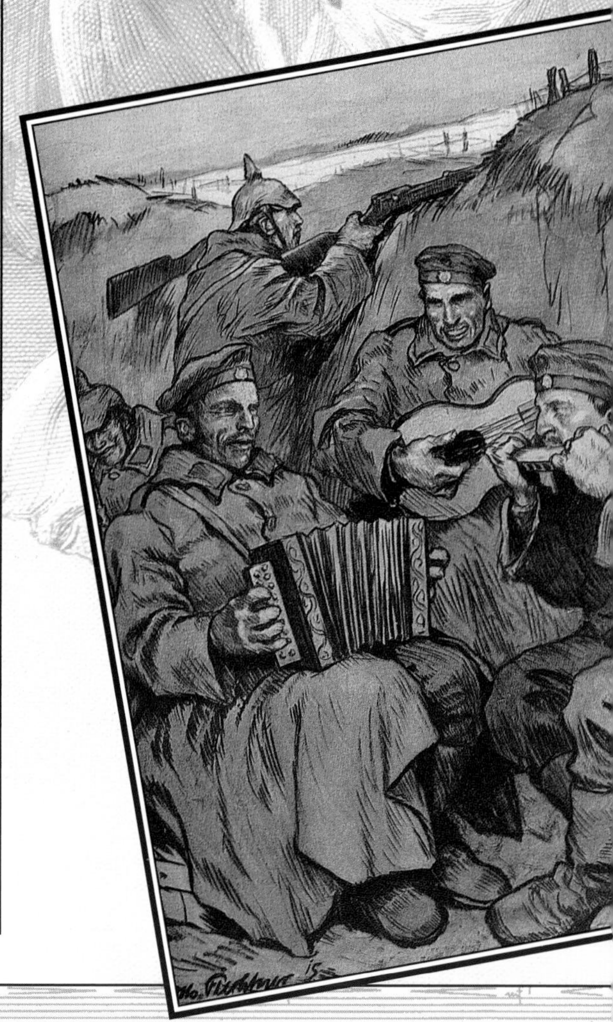

DER ROSENKAVALIER

Richard Strauss felt that for his own music, the past was as important as the future. *Der Rosenkavalier* (The Bearer of the Rose) is a romantic comedy set in the aristocratic world of 18th-century Vienna. First performed in Dresden in 1911, it was an instant and huge success. The music uses Viennese waltzes to create a world of humour, intrigue, and nostalgia – as if the violent upheavals of *Salome* and *Elektra* had never happened.

Richard Strauss (seated, centre) with colleagues

FINDING LIFE IN THE OLD WAYS

Hans Pfitzner (1869–1949) and Erich Wolfgang Korngold (1897–1957) were both conservatives at heart. Pfitzner created a masterpiece in his opera *Palestrina*, about a 16th-century Italian composer staying true to his genius despite the political and religious pressures around him. Korngold, a sensationally gifted child prodigy, was 13 when he wrote his first ballet, *Der Schneemann* (The Snowman). Alexander von Zemlinsky (1871–1942), though a traditionally minded composer, was also interested in the modernist world being explored by Mahler, and he too was a very influential conductor.

SALOME
Richard Strauss's opera, based on Oscar Wilde's play, was considered so shocking that it was banned or censored by the authorities in several cities.

FERRUCCIO BUSONI
At the turn of the century Busoni (1866–1924) was regarded as an important composer. He was also a magnificent pianist.

BREAKING WITH THE PAST

VIENNA
At the beginning of the 20th century, Vienna was the capital city of the Austro-Hungarian Empire, with a great tradition of classical music which continues to this day.

'Atonal' means 'not in any musical key'. This is still the usual description of the music that Arnold Schoenberg (1874–1951) found himself composing from 1908, rather to his own astonishment. Richard Wagner (1813–83) had lit a slow-burning fuse in his operas, whose intensity and complex chromatic harmony made them fiercely controversial works (which they still are). Fifty years on, the long-promised explosion now took place in the work of Schoenberg and his two most gifted pupils.

SCHOENBERG: THE RELUCTANT REVOLUTIONARY

Schoenberg was a gifted teacher of composition, who gave his pupils a thorough grounding in the musical styles of the past. His own music was so radical that he left tradition far behind. At the 1908 première of his Second String Quartet in Vienna, many people were appalled by its rootless, floating harmony. Others sensed the discovery of a thrilling new world.

COMRADES IN ARMS
Berg (left) and Webern were Schoenberg's two most talented pupils. Like their music, they were very different characters, but remained lifelong friends.

CITY LIFE
Vienna was an important trade and business centre, and its thriving musical life was built on this foundation of commercial strength.

HIS MASTER'S VOICE (UP TO A POINT)

Anton von Webern (1883–1945) was a student and great admirer of Schoenberg, who took his example and developed it in his own direction. Webern's music from this period is extremely spare and concentrated. For instance, his Five Pieces for Orchestra (1911–13) together last for less than five minutes.

DIFFERENT FROM THE START

Alban Berg (1885–1935), another Schoenberg pupil, briefly and not very successfully tried to work in Webern's ultra-compressed style. His music changed when Schoenberg advised him to go back to tackling larger forms. The outcome was Berg's early masterpiece, the violent and darkly coloured Three Orchestral Pieces, which were written between 1914 and 1915.

PIERROT LUNAIRE

Pierrot Lunaire is a cycle of 21 poems originally in French, exploring the disturbed mind of a moonstruck Italian clown. Using a German translation, Schoenberg set them for a singer or actress and five instrumental players. In doing so he invented the new technical device of *Sprechstimme* (literally, spoken musical voice). This searches out the indistinct boundary between singing and normal speech.

Schoenberg, a master-composer

THE VIENNA COURT OPERA HOUSE
The Viennese people were (and are) passionate about opera. What happened there made newspaper headlines, and still does.

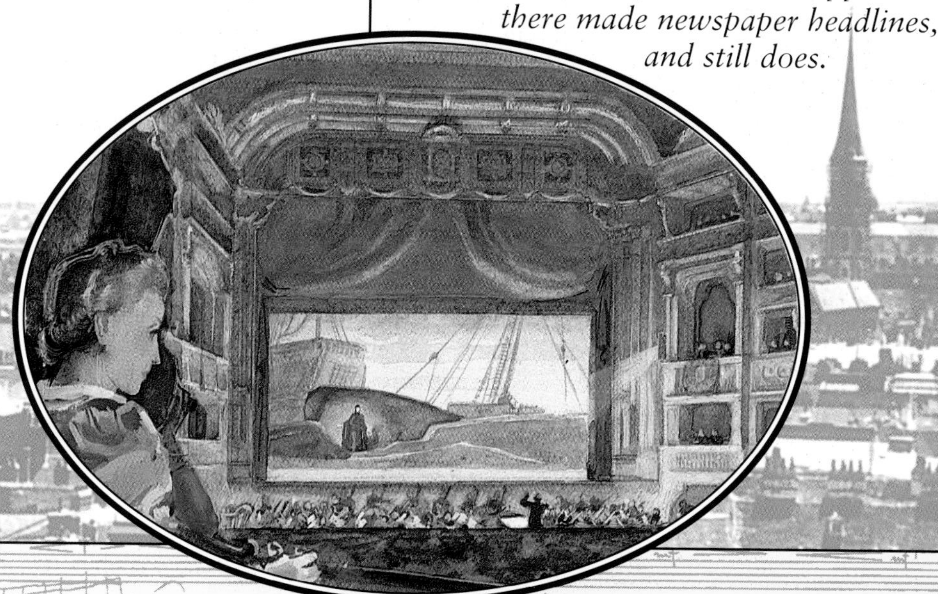

PARIS: IMPRESSIONISM AND SYMBOLISM

At the start of the new century, artistic life in Paris was the most colourful and varied in Europe. Painters, writers and composers were shaking off the academic restrictions of the past, while the city's freewheeling atmosphere attracted talent from other countries, notably the Ballets Russes company of the impresario Sergei Diaghilev.

EXOTIC APPEAL
A costume design for the Ballets Russes, the hottest ticket in town.

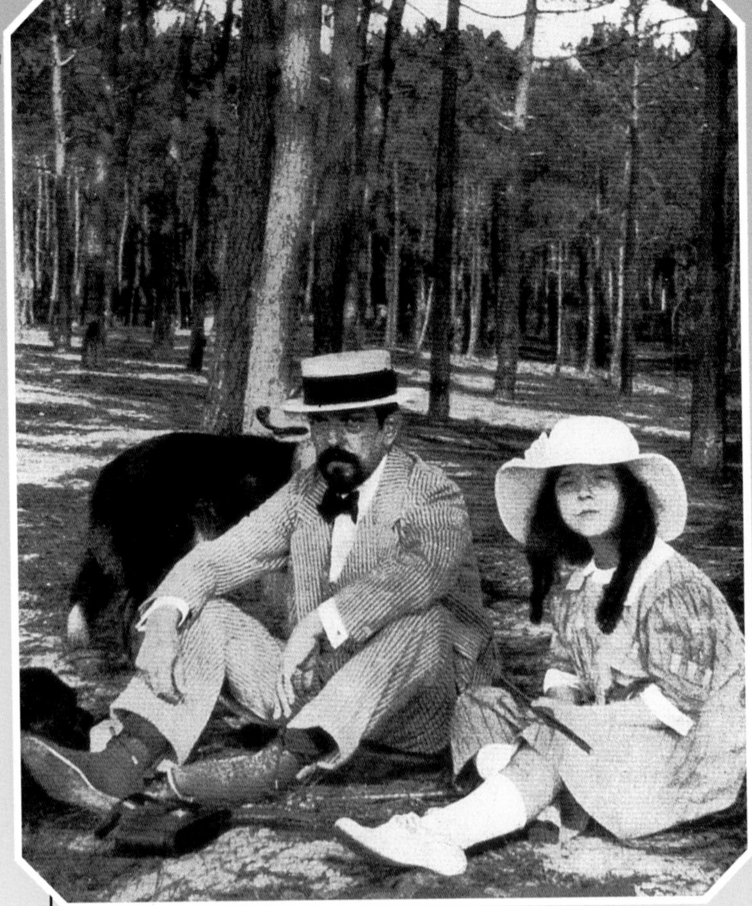

THE PROUD FATHER: CLAUDE DEBUSSY
Debussy was very fond of his daughter Claude-Emma, nicknamed Chou-Chou. In 1908, he completed Children's Corner, *six piano pieces that he dedicated to her.*

TWO QUIET REBELS
Debussy (right) believed passionately that music needed to be freed from the chains (as he saw them) of academic tradition. In this he found common ground with Erik Satie (left), whose simple but subtle compositions puzzled many concert-goers expecting something far more spectacular.

DEBUSSY: POET OF MYSTERY

The music of Claude Debussy (1862–1918) launched a quiet but bold revolution. 'In the opera house, they sing too much,' he said. So his only completed opera *Pelléas et Mélisande* (1893–1902) introduced a quite new style of composing for the stage – vivid, atmospheric and understated. In orchestral masterworks like *La Mer* (The Sea, 1905) and *Images* (1912), and also in his piano music, Debussy explored further his flair for supple rhythms and shades of instrumental colouring.

FAURE ENTERTAINS
Fauré was greatly respected by younger composers. Here, he is playing the piano at his home in Paris. On the left (with cigar) is his friend Albéniz.

RAVEL: A MASTER OF THE ORCHESTRA

Maurice Ravel (1875–1937) liked to conjure exotic sounds and ancient worlds within more sharply defined structures than Debussy, and his piano works especially are more brilliant and spectacular. His masterpiece, the ballet *Daphnis et Chloé*, set in Ancient Greece, was premièred by the Ballets Russes in 1912.

VISITORS FROM THE SOUTH

Composers from all over Europe were drawn by Paris's cosmopolitan appeal. Two Spaniards, Isaac Albéniz (1860–1909) and Manuel de Falla (1876–1946), wrote some of their finest works there (Albéniz's 12-movement cycle *Ibéria* is one of the masterpieces of Spanish piano music). Gabriel Fauré (1845–1924) was composing some of his loveliest late works. Erik Satie (1866–1925) reacted to criticism of his piano pieces ('They're shapeless,' said a reviewer) by composing more, like his *Three Pieces in the Shape of a Pear.*

ART IN PARIS

Paris was an exciting focus of developments in all the arts. The 'Impressionist' paintings of Claude Monet (1840–1926) have often been seen as the visual counterpart to the muted, half-toned atmosphere of Debussy's music. But Debussy himself preferred the work of other, different painters. He described the American James Whistler (1834–1903) as 'the greatest creator of mysterious effects in art'.

Whistler's Nocturne, blue and silver: Chelsea

FOLK SONG IN EUROPE

Much of central Europe, including what are now Hungary, Slovakia and the Czech Republic, was at this time part of the Austro-Hungarian Empire, ruled over by the Habsburg dynasty of Franz Joseph I in Vienna. Political nationalism had been growing throughout the Empire for many decades. Composers now began to reflect this in their music.

BRNO, CAPITAL OF MORAVIA
In the background (with the spire) is the Augustinian monastery, where the 11-year-old Janáček was sent to sing as a choirboy.

THE PEOPLE SING AND DANCE

The earliest works of Hungary's Béla Bartók (1881–1945) were influenced by the German concert-hall tradition of Richard Strauss. Bartók's discovery of Hungarian and Transylvanian folk music then brought about a radical change as he set about the task of cross-fertilizing these two different musical worlds within his own musical style, using dissonant harmony and driving dance-rhythms.

BARTOK AND KODALY
Bartók (seated left) and Kodály (far right) shared common musical ground in their commitment to the cause of the Hungarian people, although their own composing styles were rather different: Bartók was an instinctive modernist, Kodály more the tuneful traditionalist.

DISCONTENT IN HUNGARY
Budapest was Hungary's capital city. There, as throughout the Hungarian-speaking parts of the Habsburg Empire, political and cultural control remained mostly with German speakers appointed by Vienna. Kodály and Bartók were among those who wanted this to change.

A brilliant composer-pianist, Bartók also wrote impressively for the stage in his opera *Bluebeard's Castle* (1911) and ballets *The Wooden Prince* (1914–16) and *The Miraculous Mandarin* (1918–19).

THE COMPOSER AS TEACHER

Zoltán Kodály (1882–1967) worked together with Bartók on their travels to collect and write down the folk music they heard. The experience also influenced Kodály's own more relaxed and pictorial style. A gifted teacher, he started up a tradition of choral singing in Hungarian schools (it still thrives today) and wrote much music for it.

FROM SPEECH TO SONG

Born in the Czech region of Moravia, Leos Janáček (1854–1928) was another folk music collector. He also went further, sketching down in musical terms the everyday phrases that he heard spoken around him in the streets of the city of Brno and the Moravian countryside. 'I am trying to come close to the heart of humble Czech people,' he said. The result was a concise, vivid style of vocal writing which first flowered in his great opera *Jenufa* (1894–1903).

BELA BARTOK AT WORK
Bartók (fourth from left) travelled throughout Hungary, asking people to record their folk singing on his Edison's Phonograph, an early recording device. What he heard deeply influenced his own music.

ROMANY MUSICIANS

In the early 20th century, central Europe was still a largely rural world of poverty-entrapped villages and small towns. The mass movement of populations towards the cities and hoped-for prosperity had already begun. But while the countryside's folk music tradition was dying out, Bartók and Kodály found much of it still surviving, kept alive especially by the travelling Romany people.

Travelling folk musicians of eastern Europe

RUSSIA: REVERIE AND REVOLUTION

Imperial Russia under Tsar Nicholas II was a backward-looking, authoritarian world, whose government was finding it increasingly difficult to suppress popular demands for political change. In the same way, Russia's composers found themselves divided into those who needed no other world than the one they knew, and others who saw themselves as angry radicals.

RUSSIAN REVOLUTION

The 'first Russian Revolution' of 1905 was a surge of popular unrest following the shooting of some unarmed civilian protesters. The misery of the First World War and widespread famine finally triggered the overthrow of the Tsar in February 1917. In October, Lenin's Bolshevik Party seized power. Then followed many decades of Communist rule which would suppress the independent thought and creativity of almost all composers.

PROKOFIEV: THE YOUNG REBEL

Serge Prokofiev (1891–1953) upset his teachers at the St Petersburg Conservatory with his early, aggressively rhythmic works and the extravagant style of his Second Piano Concerto (1913). A springer of surprises, he also came up with his wry and engaging First Symphony (the 'Classical', 1918). Prokofiev decided to leave post-Revolutionary Russia for a new life in the USA in 1918.

ALEXANDER SCRIABIN
Scriabin, too, was a remarkable pianist. As a child, he practised so hard that one of his piano's pedals wore through the sole of his shoe.

PROKOFIEV THE FIREBRAND
Prokofiev was a brilliant pianist. While he was still a student, he amazed his contemporaries by composing and playing works that pushed back the boundaries of piano technique.

Revolution brews in Imperial Russia.

A LATE, GREAT ROMANTIC

The success of his Second Piano Concerto in 1901 launched Sergei Rachmaninov (1873–1943) on a triple career as a composer, conductor, and one of the century's great pianists. His music, at once passionate and melancholic, remained true to the tradition and spirit of Russian Romanticism. Rachmaninov felt that there was no place for himself or his family in post-Revolutionary Russia. He took his family with him on a tour of the Nordic countries in 1918. Later that year, they arrived in New York, to settle eventually in the USA.

A TRUE ALL-ROUNDER
Rachmaninov was music director of the Bolshoi Opera in 1904–06. Standing behind him here are two singers in the cast of his opera Francesca da Rimini *(1906).*

EXOTIC DREAMS
Léon Bakst was the Ballets Russes' acclaimed designer. This is one of his designs for a ballet based on Scheherazade *by Nikolai Rimsky-Korsakov (1844–1908), a masterpiece from 'Old' Russia.*

A COMPOSER WHO TOOK HIMSELF SERIOUSLY

Pre-Revolutionary Russia was full of strange, semi-religious cults. The composer-pianist Alexander Scriabin (1872–1915) thought of himself as a Messiah figure for future music. He wanted to build a temple in India and perform in it his *Final Mystery* for piano, massed choirs, orchestra, and an imaginary form of light-projection. Only sketches for the project survive. What might it have sounded like? Scriabin's *The Poem of Ecstasy* (1908), with its shimmering orchestration, gives an idea.

ITALY: PUCCINI AND OPERA

In Italy, opera was everything – well, almost. When the great Giuseppe Verdi (1813–1901) died, his status as the uncrowned king of Italian opera passed to Giacomo Puccini (1858–1924). Meanwhile, other composers were looking for ways of steering Italian music towards a new future.

Tragic heroine

MASCAGNI FINDS IT TOUGH AT THE TOP

Pietro Mascagni (1863–1945) claimed to be the composer who launched *verismo* (see p. 17) single-handed with *Cavalleria Rusticana* (Rustic Chivalry, 1889), his one-act opera about Sicilian peasant life. But world fame did not help him to achieve another success on anything like that scale, although his *Isabeau* (1911) and *Lodoletta* (1917) are sometimes performed today. He and Puccini once shared lodgings together, but Mascagni later became jealous of his star rival. Ruggiero Leoncavallo (1857–1919), too, never quite repeated the success of *Pagliacci* (Clowns, 1892), although his comedy *Zazà* (1900) came close.

COLLEAGUES AND RIVALS
Mascagni (left) and Puccini (right), with the composer Alberto Franchetti (1806–1942) at the piano. Puccini's career began much less successfully than Mascagni's, but he soon learned brilliantly from his mistakes.

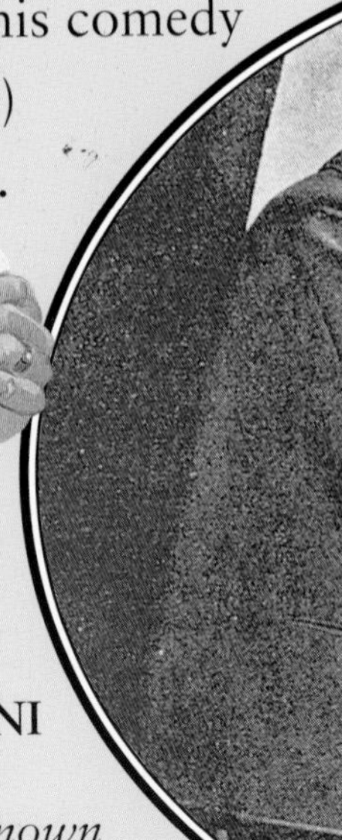

MASCAGNI
Cavalleria Rusticana *made the almost unknown Mascagni famous overnight.*

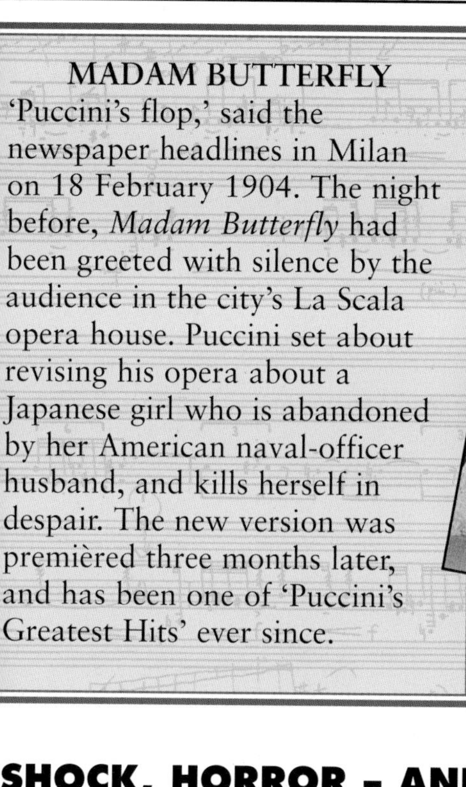

MADAM BUTTERFLY

'Puccini's flop,' said the newspaper headlines in Milan on 18 February 1904. The night before, *Madam Butterfly* had been greeted with silence by the audience in the city's La Scala opera house. Puccini set about revising his opera about a Japanese girl who is abandoned by her American naval-officer husband, and kills herself in despair. The new version was premièred three months later, and has been one of 'Puccini's Greatest Hits' ever since.

A CRUEL STORY

Puccini's Tosca *is set in 19th-century Rome. Here the heroine, Floria Tosca, watches her lover Cavaradossi (right), a political prisoner, go through what they both believe to be a mock execution by firing squad. But the bullets are real.*

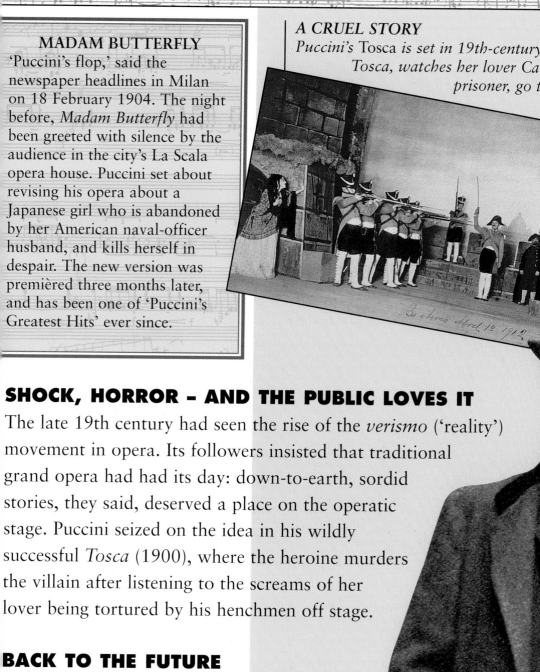

PUCCINI

In 1910, Puccini completed La Fanciulla del West *(The Girl of the Golden West) for New York's Metropolitan Opera House.*

SHOCK, HORROR – AND THE PUBLIC LOVES IT

The late 19th century had seen the rise of the *verismo* ('reality') movement in opera. Its followers insisted that traditional grand opera had had its day: down-to-earth, sordid stories, they said, deserved a place on the operatic stage. Puccini seized on the idea in his wildly successful *Tosca* (1900), where the heroine murders the villain after listening to the screams of her lover being tortured by his henchmen off stage.

BACK TO THE FUTURE

Gian Francesco Malipiero (1882–1973) was an expert in his country's rich heritage of music from previous centuries, especially the works of Claudio Monteverdi (1567–1643). This music inspired Malipiero to blend its sharply focused style of expression with modern European developments in his own compositions. Another who looked beyond Italy was Alfredo Casella (1883–1947), who was influenced by Richard Strauss and Mahler, and later by Stravinsky and Bartók.

NORDIC SYMPHONIES

Musical life in the northern European countries had always trailed behind the great powerhouses of Germany, Austria, Italy and France. Finland did not even have a symphony orchestra until 1884. Yet this small, remote country produced one of the century's greatest composers, Sibelius, and nearby Denmark gave the world Carl Nielsen.

CARL NIELSEN
Nielsen came from a poor background on the Danish island of Odense, where his father taught him to play the violin and the piano.

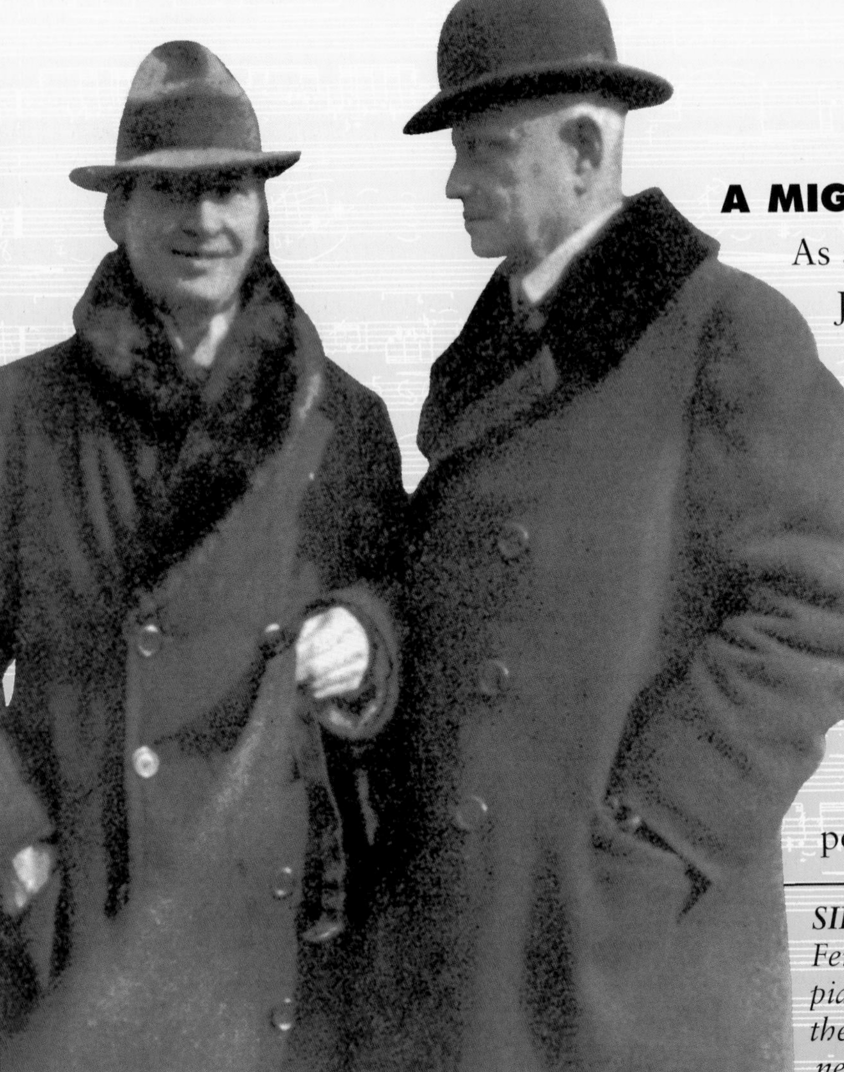

A MIGHTY VOICE FROM THE NORTH

As a young student in Helsinki, Finland, Johan Sibelius (1865–1957) dreamed of becoming a violin virtuoso. When this didn't work out, he went to study composition in Berlin and Vienna. (He later changed his name to 'Jean', in upmarket French style.) Returning to Finland, which was then part of the Russian empire, Sibelius became involved in the Finnish nationalist movement for independence. Finnish folk poetry and stories inspired his early works.

SIBELIUS WITH BUSONI
Ferruccio Busoni (left), the German-Italian compose pianist, and Sibelius were old friends. In his memoir, the English conductor Sir Henry Wood recalled: 'I never knew where they would get to...They were lik a couple of irresponsible schoolboys.'

Early successes soon made Sibelius a national hero – the tune of his symphonic poem *Finlandia* (1900), originally entitled 'Finland Awakes!', became his country's unofficial national anthem. He found fame abroad, mostly in Britain and America, with his cycle of seven symphonies.

RISING FAME
Nielsen's music started making headway outside his native Denmark. This programme of orchestral works was given at Amsterdam's famous Concertgebouw (Concert Hall) in 1912.

SYMPHONIES WITH A DIFFERENCE

Carl Nielsen (1865–1931) first earned his living as an orchestral violinist, and played in the première of his First Symphony in 1892. He became an important composer and teacher, also composing operas for the Royal Danish Theatre in Copenhagen: his comic opera *Maskarade* (1906) is regarded as Denmark's national masterpiece. Nielsen developed the unusual idea of 'progressive tonality', where a symphony travels towards an ending in a different musical key from which it began. His Fourth Symphony (1916) is subtitled 'The Inextinguishable'. 'Music is life,' Nielsen once explained. 'Like life, it cannot be extinguished.'

FAMOUS FINN
Sibelius the man brooded as darkly as some of his music. Also, he hated being photographed.

The 'Land of a Thousand Lakes'

MUSIC AND NATURE
For Sibelius, music and the Finnish landscape went together. He was able to build large musical structures out of repeated, endlessly developed fragments of melody – an idea which grew partly from his research into Finnish folk singing. The result was a spare, but highly effective technique of composing, capable of great power, and often suggesting the vast empty spaces of the snowbound Finnish countryside.

A NEW MUSIC: RAGTIME

A Blues was the original music of America's black population. It emerged from the cotton plantations of the Deep South, and made its way north to the big cities. Jazz made a similar journey, spreading out from its roots in New Orleans to conquer the world. Both were about to have a huge influence on classical music, in America and beyond.

I GOT THE BLUES

Blues allowed musicians to improvise against the fixed shapes and rhythms of verses. It flourished in vaudeville, the South's style of music-hall entertainment, and produced great singers in 'Ma' Rainey (1886–1939), Bessie Smith (1895–1937), and the unrelated Clara Smith (1894–1935).

BESSIE SMITH
At first a member of 'Ma' Rainey's vaudeville troupe, the Rabbit Foot Minstrels, Bessie Smith soon became one of the biggest blues stars in her own right, with her powerful delivery and brilliant way of timing a phrase. She died tragically in a road accident.

AHEAD OF HIS TIME
Scott Joplin is known to have heard a recording of the overture to Wagner's opera Tannhäuser. *But he was barred from hearing enough classical music to develop his composing technique, as he so wanted to.*

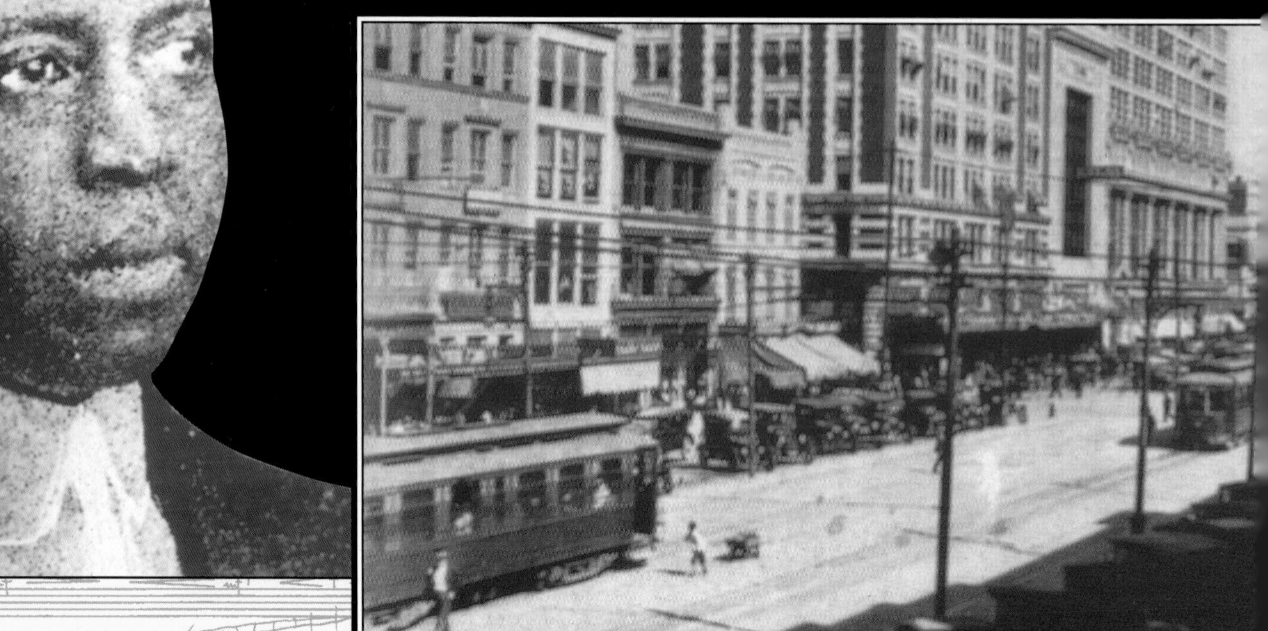

'MA' RAINEY
Born Gertrude Pridgett in Columbus, Georgia, 'Ma' Rainey took her name from her husband, vaudeville dancer William 'Pa' Rainey. She was known as 'the mother of the blues'.

A SOPHISTICATED ENTERTAINER

Ragtime was usually piano music, where the right hand played in 'ragged time' against the regular rhythmic patterns of the left (a technique known as syncopation). In Scott Joplin (1868–1917), it produced the gifted composer of *Maple Leaf Rag* and *The Entertainer*. Joplin also wrote two operas, *A Guest of Honor* (1903) and *Treemonisha* (1911), but his ambitions were thwarted by discrimination: black people were not then allowed to enter an opera house.

JAZZ SWEEPS AMERICA

The roots of jazz overlapped with those of blues and ragtime. It was played as much as sung, in bands with the trumpet, trombone and clarinet as improvising soloists and a rhythm section of guitar or banjo, drums, string bass and piano.

NEW ORLEANS
While blues originated in the cotton-growing country of the South, jazz has always been urban music. Its home was New Orleans, the colourful city in the state of Louisiana on the delta of the Mississippi River.

THE GREAT AMERICAN MUSICAL

The 'musical' had now grown from operetta and variety shows into a mix of song, story and dance. On New York's Broadway, George M. Cohan (1878–1942) wrote and directed a string of hits including *Little Johnny Jones* (1904) and *The Honeymooners* (1907). Irish-born Victor Herbert (1859–1924) wrote the songs for *Babes in Toyland* (1903), *Naughty Marietta* (1910) and others. Irving Berlin (1888–1989) became famous with his song 'Alexander's Ragtime Band' (1911) and the shows *Watch Your Step* (1914) and *Stop! Look! Listen!* (1915).

TUXEDO BAND

When the original Tuxedo Band made early recordings of jazz in 1917, the music had already travelled a long way from its origins among black Americans in the South. The Band made its name playing in New York City, and produced several musicians who went on to be jazz stars in their own right, such as Clarence Williams. Jazz was now the favourite entertainment of rich, white audiences as well as poor, black ones.

The Tuxedo Band, with Clarence Williams (bottom)

AMERICA: FROM ROMANTICISM TO IVES

Classical music in America at this time was an imported, 19th-century European product for prosperous, middle-class communities in the towns and cities. Against this conventional background, the wild originality of Charles Ives (1874–1954) came like a bolt from the blue.

EUROPEAN EXAMPLE
George W. Chadwick studied in Germany and then returned to teach music at Boston's New England Conservatory.

EUROPEAN INHERITANCE

Edward MacDowell (1860–1908) went to study piano-playing and composing in France and Germany. He then returned home and composed, played, taught at Columbia University, and relaxed by conducting a men's glee club. He was a genuinely Romantic spirit, although his music does not sound particularly American. George Chadwick (1854–1931) and Arthur Foote (1853–1937) also composed successfully within the musical forms of the European classical tradition.

HOME-GROWN TALENT
Arthur Foote studied at Harvard University with the American composer John Knowles Paine (1839–1906) and then settled in Boston, where he became an admired composer, organist and teacher.

A WOMAN COMPOSER BEFORE HER TIME

When Amy Beach (1867–1944) married at the age of 18, her husband asked her to cut down on her appearances as a brilliant concert pianist. Composing, he said, was a more suitable occupation for a married woman, and she adapted to this new life. She produced over 300 works under the name of Mrs H.H.A. Beach.

AMY BEACH

'No other life than that of a musician could ever have been possible for me,' wrote Amy Beach. Even so, it took all her determination to succeed in a man's world. It was only after her husband died, in 1910, that she was able to start touring Europe as a concert pianist. Her strongest music has real passion, although it still speaks with a European accent.

A true pioneer among composers

IVES: A NEW ENGLAND MAVERICK

Charles Ives was American classical music's first genius. The son of a bandmaster in Danbury, Connecticut, Ives took in all the different sounds of the New England world around him – hymns, popular songs and bands, besides classical music itself. Ignoring every conventional rule, he assembled his musical ideas into tapestries of sound that can be astonishingly daring and dissonant. For instance, in 'Puttnam's Camp' in *Three Places in New England* (1908–14), the orchestra imitates several bands playing at once. Ives was a partner in an insurance business, which meant that he could compose only at weekends. His music sounded very modern for its time, and only began to be properly appreciated near the end of his life. His wildly complicated *The Fourth of July* (1913) was not heard for many years. *Three Places in New England* was only premièred in 1931.

BROADWAY, NEW YORK IN 1912
Ives even tried portraying the activity of city crowds in music.

ADVENTURES IN SOUND
Ives's music explored advanced ideas like polytonality, where different sections of an orchestra play in different keys at once, like different bands being overheard outdoors at the same time. In Central Park in the Dark *(1906), orchestral sounds suggesting the quietness of the empty park itself are increasingly overlaid by noisy bursts of jazz-like music from a nearby café. These are played at the same time by a different orchestra in a different tempo, so that two conductors are needed. Nothing quite like this had ever been written down before.*

STRAVINSKY

No composer has ever leapt to fame from more unpromising beginnings than Igor Stravinsky (1882–1971). In 1909 he was an unknown former pupil of the traditionally minded Russian composer Nikolai Rimsky-Korsakov (1844–1908), who at first had not thought Stravinsky had much talent. Just four years later, Stravinsky had written three great ballet scores. Each of them unleashed a rhythmic firepower that changed western music for ever.

RURAL ROOTS
Stravinsky's love of Russian folk music started very early. Aged two, he could already accurately sing the folk songs he heard around him.

HOW TO MEET A DEADLINE

Stravinsky owed his breakthrough to Sergei Diaghilev (1872–1929), the Russian impresario who had founded the Ballets Russes company. In 1909, a commission for the company's next Paris season needed a composer at short notice. Diaghilev took a chance on Stravinsky, who worked at lightning speed and completed *The Firebird* in just five months. Based on a Russian folk tale, it was a sensational success. Stravinsky became famous overnight.

The ungainly appearance of Nijinsky's dancers was shocking.

PETRUSHKA: A PUPPET DANCES

Diaghilev wanted more 'hits', and Stravinsky provided them. In 1911, he composed the ballet *Petrushka*. Its daring use of bitonality (musical ideas in two different keys at once) broke new ground in western music. The story is about the sad love-life of a puppet (perhaps he's also human?) in a fairground show in St Petersburg. Stravinsky portrays this world in disconnected blocks of orchestral sound, held together by the rhythmic energy that drives them along. The idea was quite new. Stravinsky then took it even further.

TOP TEAM
Stravinsky (second from right, seated) with colleagues from the Ballets Russes, including the designer Léon Bakst (standing, far right).

PETRUSHKA
Stravinsky's second ballet followed a year after The Firebird.

THE RIOT OF SPRING

The first performance of *The Rite of Spring* in 1913 started the most famous riot in musical history. By the standards of classical ballet, the story was X-rated: at an imaginary ceremony, a young girl dances herself to death. The audience was outraged by the music's pounding rhythms and extreme dissonance. But after a triumphant performance the next year, Stravinsky was carried shoulder-high along the Paris streets by a crowd of admirers.

AHEAD OF ITS TIME

The audience's fury at *The Rite of Spring's* première probably related more to Nijinsky's choreography than to Stravinsky's music. In classical ballet, gravity-defying lightness is emphasized, and the dancers' feet point outwards. This picture shows that Nijinsky had them doing the opposite, as he tried to convey the music's earth-stamping power in visual terms. He had begun to invent modern dance.

VASLAV NIJINSKY
Nijinsky (illustrated here by Georges Barbier in 1913) was the most gifted dancer of his day, and the Ballets Russes' biggest draw. He also had bold and experimental ambitions as a choreographer. His virtuoso performance in Petrushka's *title role was the talk of Paris in the summer of 1911.*

ENGLAND: SUNSET AND DAWN

At the start of the 20th century Britain had an empire on which, it was proudly said, 'the sun never sets'. But England's composers preferred to stand aside from this apparently secure and serene world (which was soon to be engulfed in mechanized war). Some reacted against it, and turned instead to their country's musical grass roots for ideas and inspiration.

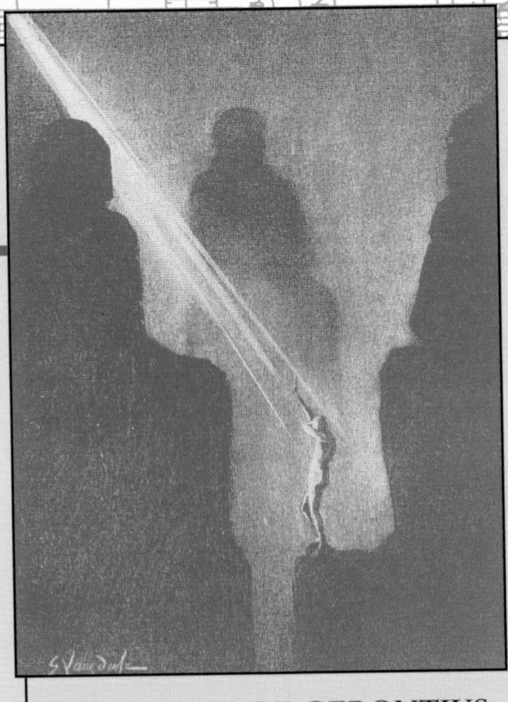

THE DREAM OF GERONTIUS
Elgar's oratorio is now one of his most loved works, but at its first performance, the choir and players found the music strange and difficult. The illustration above portrays the journey of Gerontius's soul after death towards the sight of God.

POMP AND CIRCUMSTANCE (ON THE OUTSIDE ONLY)

The proud Empire itself seemed to speak through the most popular music of Edward Elgar (1857–1934), like his *Pomp and Circumstance Marches* (the tune of 'Land of Hope and Glory' comes from one of them). But the real Elgar is found in much larger and deeper works such as the oratorio *The Dream of Gerontius* (1900) and his two symphonies. They contain dark warnings of upheavals to come, alongside the inner strength that Elgar drew from his Catholic faith.

ELGAR IN THE STUDIO
Elgar was interested in gramophone recordings, and made some of the very earliest ones. The device in front of him funnelled the sound of the orchestra towards a microphone.

GO WEST, YOUNG MAN

The young Frederick Delius (1862–1934) was sent by his father to Florida to manage an orange grove. Delius's music was marked for life by the tropical glow of his surroundings and the sound of black male voices singing as they worked. Returning to Europe and living mostly in France, he produced two radiant masterworks in his opera *A Village Romeo and Juliet* (1901), a tragic story of young love, set in Switzerland, and his anti-religious oratorio *A Mass of Life* (1905).

A POET IN SOUND
Delius had strong links with the cultures of Germany and Scandinavia. The mountain landscapes of Norway inspired his A Song of the High Hills *(1911) for wordless chorus and orchestra.*

THE PLANETS

Gustav Holst (1874–1934) and Vaughan Williams shared a common interest in the folk music they collected together. But Holst also had more exotic interests, like the astrological star-signs that inspired his orchestral suite *The Planets* (1914–17). Many believed that the battering rhythms of its opening movement, *Mars, the Bringer of War,* were a vision of the First World War, but Holst always denied this.

TWENTY·TWO·PENCE
THE·PLANETS·SUITE
Gustav Holst

A postage stamp, commemorating Holst's most famous work

THE COUNTRYSIDE ENDURES

Aiming to renew the deepest values of English music, Ralph Vaughan Williams (1872–1958) went back to basics in a different way. He edited English hymn tunes, researched English music of earlier centuries, and collected folk songs in the English countryside. He combined all these influences in works like the *Fantasia on a Theme of Thomas Tallis* (1910) and *The Lark Ascending* (1914). *A Sea Symphony* (1909) is a choral setting of words by the American poet Walt Whitman.

Gustav Holst

MASTERPIECES
Holst (left) also composed Savitri *(1908), a chamber opera on a Hindu story, and* The Hymn of Jesus *(1917) for chorus and orchestra.*

WAR DESTROYS THE OLD WORLD

The First World War broke out in August 1914. When it ended over four years later, Europe was a different place. The defeated German and Austro-Hungarian empires were broken up by Britain and France, the exhausted victors, while Russia descended into the chaos of revolution. The lives of composers were changed like everyone else's.

A GENIUS REGROUPS AND STARTS AGAIN

Stravinsky was marooned during the war in the neutral country of Switzerland. Wartime conditions meant that the lavish productions of the Ballets Russes were no longer possible. So Stravinsky struck out in a new direction, writing works for much smaller forces. He arranged Russian folk songs, and sketched out a Russian ballet *Les Noces* (The Wedding, 1914–17). *Renard* (The Fox, 1916) was a bolder idea: a story about farmyard animals, portrayed by singers and acrobats.

THE SOLDIER'S TALE

Working with the Swiss poet C.F. Ramuz, Stravinsky composed *The Soldier's Tale* (1918) for a travelling theatre group. The story – about a soldier who sells his soul to the devil as the price of love and riches – is portrayed by actors, a dancer, and a group of seven musicians. Out of the blue, Stravinsky had come up with the first example of what we now call music theatre.

Stravinsky (seated) visiting Debussy

CALLED UP

Schoenberg spent the war in and out of the Austrian army, although he was not sent to the front. Webern constantly petitioned the authorities to exempt Schoenberg from military duty, because of his former teacher's national importance as a composer.

LIFE AT THE FRONT

Pictures like this one (probably posed) suggested that in the First World War, the front line wasn't such a bad place to be. In reality the mechanized slaughter, poison gas and mud were a nightmare, from which Europe has perhaps never quite recovered.

SITTING IT OUT
Richard Strauss composed busily during the war years. Besides his work on the vast score of Die Frau ohne Schatten, *he wrote a chamber opera,* Ariadne auf Naxos *(Ariadne on Naxos), which was premièred in 1916.*

STAIRWAY TO HEAVEN

Like his pupils Webern and Berg, Schoenberg was called up into the Austrian army. Between on-off periods of wartime service he set about composing *Die Jakobsleiter* (Jacob's Ladder, 1917). This was planned as a vast oratorio, about the meeting of heaven and Earth which the biblical figure of Jacob saw in a dream. Schoenberg never completed it, but even so, the unfinished oratorio is one of his greatest achievements.

DIFFERENT RESPONSES

When the war broke out, Ravel quickly completed one of his finest works, his Piano Trio (1914). He then joined up, driving a military ambulance at the Western Front, where the German army had invaded France. Increasingly ill with cancer, Debussy wrote a brilliant set of piano *Etudes* (Studies, 1915) before his death in 1918. Richard Strauss, living at his mountain home in German Bavaria, went on composing almost as if the war wasn't happening. In 1919 he completed his grandest opera, *Die Frau ohne Schatten* (The Woman without a Shadow).

ON SERVICE
Ravel felt it his duty to serve his country during the war, although he had to stop composing for a time.

Glossary

Atonality A term meaning 'music in no key', often describing the work of Schoenberg and his followers. Schoenberg preferred 'pantonality' (music in all keys at once).

Chromatic (from the Greek word *chromatikos*, 'coloured') Used to describe music whose different harmonies are more extreme than those of earlier composers, such as Mozart.

Concerto A work for solo instruments and orchestra.

Dissonant (or 'discordant') Two or more notes which, when played together, produce a harsh, unstable sound.

Glee club An amateur group for singing unaccompanied songs in England and America.

Improvised Music which is not written down, but composed at the moment it is performed.

Key The bedrock idea of classical music, where the harmony sounds fixed to a particular 'keynote'.

Modernism A term which loosely describes music that sounds modern compared to earlier music.

Oratorio A setting of a text on a religious subject, for solo voices, chorus and orchestra.

Piano trio A work for a violin, cello and piano.

Soprano The highest type of female voice.

String quartet A work for four stringed instruments: two violins, viola and cello. Also the group that plays it.

Symphonic poem A work for orchestra, usually in a single movement (section), telling a story or depicting a particular scene (say in a city or the countryside). Sometimes referred to as a 'Tone poem' (a mistranslation of the German word *Tondichtung*, which means 'sound-poem').

Symphony Traditionally, an orchestral work in four movements. By the 20th century this form could be much expanded to include several more movements, sometimes also using solo and choral voices. There are also one-movement symphonies.

Waltz A swirling ballroom dance, in rhythmic units of three beats. Waltzes were much loved in Vienna.

WORLD EVENTS

- *'Boxer' Rebellion in China*
- *First transatlantic radio transmission*
- *Boer War ends in South Africa*
- *First powered flight, by the Wright brothers*
- *Start of Russo-Japanese War*
- *First Revolution in Russia*
- *San Francisco earthquake*
- *Maiden voyage of the liner* Lusitania
- *Henry Ford launches the Model T motor car*
- *Blériot is the first to fly from England to France*
- *Japan annexes Korea*
- *Chinese Revolution deposes the Emperor*
- *The liner* Titanic *sinks*
- *Henry Ford invents the assembly line*
- *First World War breaks out*
- *ANZAC defeat at Gallipoli, Turkey*
- *Easter Rising in Dublin*
- *Russian Revolutions in February and October*
- *End of First World War*
- *Treaty of Versailles*

TIMELINE

	MUSICAL EVENTS	THE ARTS	FAMOUS MUSICIANS	MUSICAL WORKS
00	•Première of Leoncavallo's Zazà	•Death of Oscar Wilde, Irish writer	•Birth of Aaron Copland, American composer	•Mahler's Fourth Symphony
01	•Rachmaninov plays Second Piano Concerto	•Buddenbrooks, first novel by Thomas Mann	•Birth of Jascha Heifetz, American violinist	•Elgar's Pomp and Circumstance March No. 1
02	•First recordings by Enrico Caruso	•Heart of Darkness, novella by Joseph Conrad	•Birth of jazz clarinettist Omer Simeon	•Pélleas et Mélisande, opera by Debussy
03	•Janáček completes his third opera, Jenufa	•Call of the Wild by novelist Jack London	•Birth of jazz drummer Ben Pollack	•Pelleas und Melisande, this time by Schoenberg
04	•Puccini's Madam Butterfly flops in Milan	•Chekhov's The Cherry Orchard first staged	•Birth of Coleman Hawkins, jazz saxophonist	•Debussy's L'Isle Joyeuse for piano
05	•Lehár's operetta The Merry Widow premièred	•Exhibition of 'Fauvist' art at Paris's Salon d'Automne	•Birth of bandleader Cecil Scott	•Richard Strauss's opera Salome
06		•Death of Henrik Ibsen, Norwegian dramatist	•Birth of Shostakovich, Russian composer	•Schoenberg's First Chamber Symphony
07	•Janáček completes his opera Osud	•Picasso paints Les Demoiselles d'Avignon	•Death of Edvard Grieg, Norwegian composer	•Sibelius's Third Symphony
08	•Schoenberg's first atonal works	•Formation of the 'Ashcanners' artists	•Birth of Olivier Messiaen, French composer	•Mahler's Das Lied von der Erde
09	•First appearance of the Ballets Russes in Paris	•Italy's Futurist movement publishes its manifesto	•Birth of jazz musician Gil Rodin	•Webern's Six Orchestral Pieces, Op. 6
0	•Stravinsky's The Firebird premièred	•First abstract paintings by Wassily Kandinsky	•Birth of Art Tatum, American jazz pianist	•Alban Berg's String Quartet, Op. 3
1	•First performance of Der Rosenkavalier	•Birth of Elizabeth Bishop, American poet	•Death of Mahler	•Berlin's 'Alexander's Ragtime Band'
2	•Ravel's ballet Daphnis et Chloé premièred	•Death of August Strindberg, Swedish writer	•Birth of John Cage, American composer	•Schoenberg's melodrama Pierrot Lunaire
3	•Riot at Stravinsky's ballet The Rite of Spring	•First International Exhibition of Modern Art	•Birth of Benjamin Britten, British composer	•Debussy completes his ballet Jeux
4	•Opening of Berlin's Watch Your Step	•Publication of adventure story Tarzan of the Apes	•Birth of Billie Holiday, American blues singer	•Vaughan Williams's The Lark Ascending
5		•The Rainbow, novel by D.H. Lawrence published	•Birth of Frank Sinatra, American singer	•Debussy composes two sets of Etudes for piano
6	•Première of Strauss's Ariadne auf Naxos	•Monet paints series of Water Lilies	•Birth of Yehudi Menuhin, American violinist	•Nielsen's Fourth Symphony
7	•Original Dixieland Jazz Band's first recordings	•Dutch avant-garde artists publish magazine De Stijl	•George M. Cohan publishes 'Over There'	•Schoenberg sketches out oratorio Die Jakobsleiter
8	•Louis Armstrong plays with King Oliver's band	•Lytton Strachey publishes Eminent Victorians	•Birth of Leonard Bernstein, composer	•Stravinsky completes The Soldier's Tale
9		•Bauhaus school of art and architecture opens	•Birth of Margot Fonteyn, ballerina	•Richard Strauss completes Die Frau ohne Schatten

INDEX

National
4 & 5

Modern Studies

Social Issues in the UK

Frank Cooney
Paul Creaney
Alison Elliott

HODDER GIBSON
AN HACHETTE UK COMPANY

The Publishers would like to thank the following for permission to reproduce copyright material:

Photo credits p.6 © Ross McDairmant/Rex Features; p.8 © F. Schussler/Photodisc/Getty Images / Background Objects V08; p.9 © TopFoto.co.uk; p.10 © WWW.SCOTTISHVIEWPOINT.COM; p.16 © Scott Griessel – Fotolia.com; p.17 © 1997 Jules Frazier/Photodisc/ Getty Images/ Eat, Drink, Dine 48; p.18 © Photofusion Picture Library / Alamy; p.19 © Ray Tang/Rex Features; p.20 © AFP/Getty Images; p.22 © Kelpfish – Fotolia.com; p.26 © Getty Images; p.27 © Les Gibbon / Alamy; p.29 (top) © 2006 Getty Images, (bottom) © DAILY RECORD / Mirrorpix; p.32 © Danny Lawson/PA Archive/Press Association Images; p.33 © By Ian Miles-Flashpoint Pictures / Alamy; p.38 © Andrew Milligan/PA Archive/Press Association Images; p.41 © Andrew Milligan/PA Archive/Press Association Images; p.44 © Getty Images; p.46 © Children's Hearings Scotland (www.chscotland.gov.uk/); p.54 © Justin Kase zsixz / Alamy; p.56 © britstock images ltd / Alamy; p.57 © Vitalinko – Fotolia.com; p.58 © manipulateur - Fotolia.com; p.64 © Alan Wilson / Alamy; p.70 (left) © MARK DUFFY / Alamy, (right) © Conservative Party; p.73 (left) © Allstar Picture Library / Alamy, (right) © Andrew Milligan/PA Wire/Press Association Images; p.86 © ACE STOCK LIMITED / Alamy; p.88 © Bubbles Photolibrary; p.94 © SHOUT / Alamy; p.95 © BMI Ross Hall Hospital; p.97 © Christopher Dodge – Fotolia.com; p.99 © Petro Feketa – Fotolia.com; p.103 © Frank Cooney; p.104 © Frank Cooney; p.106 © Frank Cooney.

Acknowledgements The text extract on p.6 is reproduced with permission of Herald & Times Group. From *Herald Scotland*, 'New football laws hailed a success', Monday 5 November 2012. The text extract on p.21 has been quoted from the *Guardian*, 'Were the riots about race?', Thursday 8 December 2011. Copyright Guardian News & Media Ltd 2011. The text extract on p.69 is reproduced courtesy of the British Association for Supported Employment (http://base-uk.org). The text extract on p.71 is reproduced with permission of Herald & Times Group. From *Sunday Herald*, 'Sturgeon unveils panel to find "Scottish values" alternative to Westminster benefit cuts', Sunday 6 January 2013. The text extract on p.76 is reproduced with permission of Citizens Advice Scotland. The information is correct at time of publication – please visit www.adviceguide.org.uk for the latest, up-to-date information. The text extract on p.81 is reproduced with permission of the Scottish Council for Voluntary Organisations. Extracts from the National 4 Modern Studies Course Specification (p.108), National 4 Added Value Unit Specification (p.111), National 5 Modern Studies Course Specification (p.113) and National 5 Modern Studies Course Support Notes (p.118) are reproduced with the permission of the Scottish Qualifications Authority.

Orders: please contact Bookpoint Ltd, 130 Park Drive, Milton Park, Abingdon, Oxon OX14 4SE. Telephone: (44) 01235 827720. Fax: (44) 01235 400454. Lines are open 9.00–5.00, Monday to Saturday, with a 24-hour message answering service. Visit our website at www.hoddereducation.co.uk. Hodder Gibson can be contacted direct on: Tel: 0141 333 4650; Fax: 0141 404 8188; email: hoddergibson@ hodder.co.uk

First published in 2013 by

Hodder Gibson, an imprint of Hodder Education,
An Hachette UK Company
211 St Vincent Street
Glasgow G2 5QY

Impression number 5 4

Year 2017

Cover photo © Epicscotland/Alamy

Illustrations by Emma Golley at Redmoor Design and Integra Software Services Pvt. Ltd

Typeset in 11 on 14pt ITC Stone Serif Medium by Integra Software Services Pvt. Ltd., Pondicherry, India.

Printed in Dubai

A catalogue record for this title is available from the British Library

ISBN: 978 1 4441 8224 8

Contents

Section 1 Crime and the law

Section 2 Social inequality

Chapter 1

What is crime?

What is crime?

Crime is ...

Show your understanding

Branch out

1 This question, what is crime, is more complicated than you might think. Discuss in class and come up with a working definition of what is meant by 'crime'.

Why are rules and laws necessary?

Rights and responsibilities are an important part of a democracy. Rules and laws are necessary to ensure that people's rights are respected. We have rules in our homes, at school and in the workplace to ensure we live in as safe environments as possible.

Most people accept that rules and laws are necessary to prevent a complete breakdown of law and order (anarchy).

Show your understanding

Branch out

1 Group activity
Have a discussion about what it would be like if we lived in 'a state of nature', that is, with no rules or laws.

What you will learn:

1 What crime is.
2 Who is responsible for deciding what is criminal.
3 About the different types of crime.
4 Trends in crime statistics.

Crime takes place when the laws of a country are broken. It is the job of the police to prevent crime and to investigate cases of law-breaking.

Who is responsible for deciding what is criminal?

Scots law

Scotland has its own distinct legal system. The UK and Scottish Parliaments make laws called Acts of Parliament which the people of Scotland and the United Kingdom should obey. The courts in Scotland can change the law. The UK Parliament makes laws on behalf of the Scottish people on what are called reserved matters, for example finance, the economy, energy and transport; the Scottish Parliament makes laws on devolved matters such as education, health, and law and order issues.

Scottish Parliament's new powers

The Scotland Act (2012) gave the Scottish Parliament various new powers, including law-making powers over air weapons in Scotland and responsibility for drink driving limits and speed limits on Scotland's roads.

New laws are continually passed, such as the 2006 banning of smoking in public places. This was resented by many smokers but the decision was supported by the majority of the Scottish public. A controversial law to reinforce laws against **bigotry** was enacted in 2012 (see Case study below).

Bigotry: intolerance towards those who hold different opinions from oneself (this can include intolerance of different religious beliefs, political opinions or racial backgrounds).

Case study: New crimes

Football Banning Orders

The Police, Public Order and Criminal Justice (Scotland) Act 2006 included the introduction of Football Banning Orders (FBOs). If subject to a FBO, a person is banned from attending football matches and from attending public houses where a live match is being shown. FBOs are intended for those involved in serious and violent behaviour.

The Offensive Behaviour at Football and Threatening Communications (Scotland) Act 2012 was passed by the Scottish Parliament on 14 December 2011 to further strengthen laws against bigotry. The Act, which came into force in March 2012, criminalises behaviour which is threatening, hateful or otherwise offensive at a regulated football match including offensive singing or chanting. It also applies to behaviour on the way to football matches at all levels and also where football matches are being broadcast, except in domestic property. It also criminalises the communication of threats of serious violence and threats intended to incite religious hatred, whether sent through the post or posted on the Internet. Penalties range from fixed penalty notices (£40) and Community Payback Orders to an unlimited fine and five years in prison. (See also pages 11–12.)

LEGISLATION INTRODUCED TO TACKLE FOOTBALL VIOLENCE AND DISORDER HAS BEEN HAILED A SUCCESS BY PROSECUTORS

Since the Offensive Behaviour at Football and Threatening Communications (Scotland) Act 2012 was introduced on 1 March, 89% of reported cases of offensive behaviour have been prosecuted and 83% of those have led to convictions. In relation to reports of threatening communications, 78% of cases were prosecuted.

A football banning order can be applied to conduct relating to a football match rather than football in general.

A Scottish Government spokesman said: 'We've made clear that bigotry and hatred will not be tolerated and have brought in legislation to give police and prosecutors additional tools in their armoury to punish those who carry out this behaviour.'

Adapted from www.heraldscotland.com, 5 November 2012

Figure 1.1 Some supporters of Celtic and Rangers football clubs feel they are being victimised and may end up with a criminal record if charged and found guilty of singing offensive chants

Criminal law and civil law

Criminal law deals with identifying when the law has been broken and with prosecuting offenders. There are different levels of severity of crime from driving offences to rape and murder. Civil law is used to settle disputes between individuals and organisations. It sets out rules for civil procedures such as buying or selling a house. Civil law affects our daily lives, personal relationships within families and among neighbours. For example, if there was a dispute over a tree blocking light into a neighbour's house, it would be dealt with by civil law.

Show your understanding

Branch out

1 Working in pairs, use each of the categories of crime in the box above as a heading: sort the following crimes under the relevant heading(s). (Note: some of the crimes may be able to be placed under more than one heading.)

- Illegal use of a firearm
- Verbal racist abuse
- Violence towards spouse
- Computer hacking
- Burglary
- Tax avoidance
- Dealing in illegal substances
- Shoplifting
- Copyright theft
- Identity theft
- Homicide
- Assault
- Mugging
- Graffiti
- Vandalism
- Driving without a licence
- Selling alcohol to people under the legal age
- Mis-selling insurance
- Online tax fraud
- **Botnets**
- Stranded traveller scams
- Online banking fraud

Different types of crime

Types of crime

There are different types of crime. Often crimes are categorised under broad headings such as:

- White-collar crime
- Blue-collar crime
- Corporate crime
- Crime of hatred
- Cybercrime
- Domestic abuse
- Crimes involving fire
- Violent crime

White-collar crime

The term 'white-collar' refers to employees who work in offices and sales and who do not work in manual labour. The first person to use the term white-collar crime was a sociologist called Edwin Sutherland. He described it as 'a crime committed by a person of respectability in the course of his occupation'. White-collar crime includes fraud, bribery and money laundering. These are often hidden crimes as many firms choose not to report the crime to the police and prefer to deal with the problem internally.

White-collar crime costs UK companies an estimated £4 billion a year. Think how many people's jobs this is equivalent to.

Show your understanding

Branch out

1 Through discussion in class and/or by searching the Internet, find out more types of white-collar crime.

Botnet: A botnet is a collection of Internet-connected computers whose security defences have been breached and are now controlled by an individual or a group intending to cause damage to computer systems. Each affected computer is known as a 'bot'.

FACT FILE

Pensions fraud

A recent example of serious white-collar crime that has affected many innocent and vulnerable people is pensions fraud.

'Pensions fraud is one of the biggest threats to individuals. That's the warning today from the joint Head of Fraud at the Serious Fraud Office. The SFO believes hundreds of millions of pounds of pension money has been targeted by suspected fraudsters, leaving thousands of customers without their funds. The scam begins by getting individuals to transfer their money from their pension scheme into a self-invested personal pension – a SIPP. The crooks then persuade the individual to transfer that money abroad where it disappears.'

Quoted from www.bbc.co.uk/programmes/b01l94zy

Blue-collar crime

A blue-collar worker is a member of the working class who performs manual labour, which may involve skilled or unskilled jobs such as in the construction industry. Blue-collar work often involves a product physically being built, manufactured or maintained. Blue-collar crime tends to be more obvious than white-collar crime, for example housebreaking, vandalism and selling stolen goods.

Although the percentage of white-collar criminals has risen, numbers still show a large majority of prisoners are poor, blue-collar criminals. One reason for this is that blue-collar crimes tend to be more obvious and attract more police attention. It is often difficult to detect white-collar crime because it is usually linked to a person's everyday work and can go unseen. Also, blue-collar crime is more likely to involve physical force, either through breaking and entering or assault so is more likely to be punished by imprisonment.

Show your understanding

Branch out

1 Why do you think there is less research into white-collar crime?

Violent crime

Robbery is different from theft in that it involves taking something from a person by force, intimidation or by threatening to use force, such as mugging, carjacking and armed robbery.

When a person is beaten up or threatened with violence, this is known as assault. Assault that is motivated by racism, homophobia or religious hatred can result in more serious punishment.

Domestic violence includes violent or aggressive behaviour between people in a family or in a relationship, including child abuse. Unfortunately, many victims of domestic violence do not report these crimes; they may feel it's their own fault or be too ashamed to seek help.

Knife crime

Knife crime includes:

- Carrying or trying to buy a knife if you are under 18
- Threatening people with a knife
- Carrying a knife that is banned
- A murder where the victim was stabbed with a knife
- A robbery or burglary where the thieves carried a knife as a weapon

While there has been a lot of news coverage of knife crimes recently, this type of crime still makes up a small percentage of the total crimes in the UK. However, the extent of the injuries possible makes it a very serious issue (see pages 29–30).

Figure 1.2 Knife crime makes up a small percentage of the total crimes in the UK

Gun crime

Gun crime includes any crime that involves the use of a gun or a firearm. This also includes carrying or using an imitation gun.

Human trafficking

- Between 2007 and 2008, 79 victims of human trafficking came into contact with the authorities.
- The main trafficking route to Scotland is via London.
- The majority of cases were females who had been trafficked into sexual exploitation.
- A minority were trafficked into other industries.

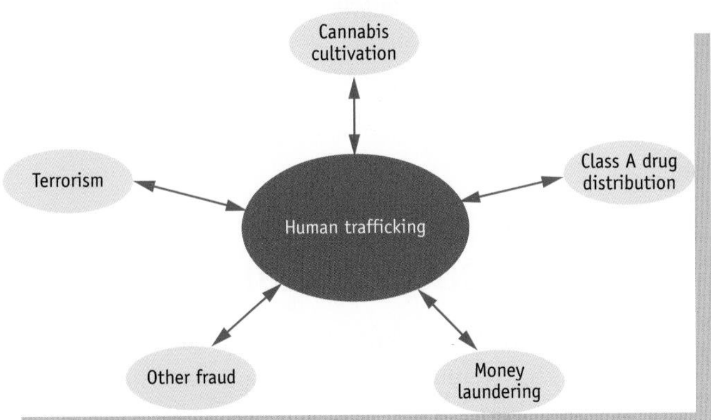

Source: Human Trafficking in Scotland 2007–2008

Figure 1.3 Links between human trafficking and other forms of serious organised crime

Crimes of dishonesty

Crimes of dishonesty include housebreaking, theft from a motor vehicle, shoplifting and fraud.

Anti-social behaviour

Anti-social behaviour can make people feel very uncomfortable living in their communities. It includes noisy neighbours, graffiti, intimidation and vandalism.

Figure 1.4 Drugs seized by the Metropolitan Police's Flying Squad as they foiled an armed robbery

Drug crimes

Category of drug	For possession	For production or supply
Class A Heroin, cocaine, LSD, morphine, ecstasy, methadone	Up to 7 years in prison or an unlimited fine (or both)	Up to life imprisonment or an unlimited fine (or both)
Class B Speed, cannabis, amphetamine, dihydrocodeine	Up to 5 years in prison or an unlimited fine (or both)	Up to 14 years' imprisonment or an unlimited fine (or both)
Class C GHB, temazepam, valium, tamgesic	Up to 2 years in prison or an unlimited fine (or both) (applies to valium and temazepam if acquired without a prescription)	Up to 14 years' imprisonment or an unlimited fine (or both)

Table 1.1 Categories of drug and maximum sentences for possession and production or supply

Racial hate crime

Race crime is described as 'racially aggravated' or 'racially motivated' and includes crimes committed on the basis of race, nationality, culture and language. This type of crime can cause a lot of fear in communities.

Race crime does not necessarily involve violence or physical injury. It could be in the form of threatening or abusive language. If a crime is racially motivated it can carry a stiffer sentence than if the same crime was committed with no racial motive (see also page 24).

FACT FILE

- The number of racist incidents recorded by the police in Scotland has increased for the first time in five years with 5,389 incidents recorded in 2011–12.
- This is 10% higher than the 4,911 incidents recorded in 2010–11.
- Of those who were victims of a racist incident, 34% were aged 26 to 35 years, compared with 13% who were aged 20 or under.
- Males were more likely to be a victim of a racist incident (17 per 10,000 population) than females (6 per 10,000 population).

Source: Scottish Government

Figure 1.5 Shops owned by and serving the Asian community in Scotland

RACIAL ASSAULT

In January 2013 Paige Bain, 16, and her aunt Eileen Kennedy, 28, were found guilty of two racially aggravated assaults. They punched two black African ladies while uttering racial abuse. The attack took place in a playpark in the Royston area of Glasgow. Bain was sentenced to 980 days in jail and Kennedy 726 days.

Data collected	Financial year				
	2004–05	2006–07	2008–09	2010–11	2011–12
Incidents	4,519	5,322	5,145	4,911	5,389
Crimes	5,734	6,654	6,617	6,173	6,472
Victims	5,059	5,963	5,995	5,906	6,311
Perpetrators	3,321	5,082	5,447	5,562	5,281

Source: Scottish Government

Table 1.2 Racist incidents in Scotland

Crime aggravated by religious prejudice

Section 74 of the *Criminal Justice (Scotland) Act 2003* states that 'an offence is aggravated by religious prejudice where the alleged conduct was aggravated by some form of malice or ill will based on the victim's membership of a religious group'. This is called sectarianism.

FACT FILE

In the year 2011–12, there were arrests for sectarian offences in all of Scotland's 32 local authorities.

- While arrests fell in Glasgow, Glasgow still accounts for 40% of the total.
- In Edinburgh religiously aggravated offences more than doubled between 2011 and 2012.
- Overall the number rose from 693 charges in 2010–11 to 876 charges in 2011–12: a 26% increase.
- The police were the most common target in both periods 2010–11 and 2011–12.
- Workers such as hospital staff, security staff and taxi drivers were targeted in 13% of incidents.
- In the period 2010–11, 57.7% (400) of charges were as a result of offences targeting Roman Catholicism. This rose during the period 2011–12 to 58.1% (509).
- In the period 2010–11 36.5% (253) of charges were as a result of offences targeting Protestantism. This rose during the period 2011–12 to 40% (353).
- There was a rise in offences targeting Islam, from 15 (2.1%) to 19 (2.2%).
- More than 25% of anti-Islam charges were for assaults.
- 93% of accused were male.
- 58% of accused were aged between 16 and 30.

Source: The *Herald*, 24 November 2012

Viewpoints of groups and individuals

Anti-sectarian charity Nil By Mouth

The Nil By Mouth charity points out that the problem goes beyond football. Although the problems relating to football rose, the problems inside stadia decreased. Nil By Mouth emphasises that most incidents took place on public transport, streets and residential areas, leading to a call for a nationwide rehabilitation scheme for offenders.

Catholic Church

The Catholic Church said that there had to be a 'public acknowledgement of the extent of anti-Catholicism in Scotland'. Archbishop Philip Tartaglia said, 'Sadly, it seems incontrovertible now that our problem is not so much sectarianism but anti-Catholicism.'

The Church of Scotland

The Church of Scotland's Sectarianism report from May 2012 reiterates their 2002 report that 'Sectarianism is not someone else's problem, it's an issue for us all.'

The report mentions the work of Nil By Mouth Charter for Change, that sectarianism is not just about football, it's about the small asides and bigoted jokes and will continue to be pervasive in Scottish society unless we acknowledge all of this as a society.

This report acknowledges projects tackling sectarianism, such as Bridging the Gap.

'Bridging the Gap was set up by Blessed John Duns Scotus Church and Gorbals Parish Church to bring the two denominations (Protestant and Catholic) closer together to

work across divides in the community. Originally the work addressed sectarianism and divides between generations and now it has been extended to work with asylum seekers, welcoming them and helping them to integrate into the area. The project is a visible sign that there is Christian unity with a focus on enhancing the lives of all the people in the community. This is a formal way of demonstrating commitment to one another, which is more than just about inter-church relationships.

'Some of the work has involved relationships with local schools. There is a peer tutoring system in the two local high schools – one Roman Catholic the other non-denominational. S4 pupils help P7s from the nine primary schools in South Glasgow that feed into the two high schools.

'In 2011, Bridging the Gap took 90 S4 pupils to Northern Ireland where there is a twinning arrangement with a school in West Belfast.'

Rape and sexual assault

Rape is when someone forces another person to have sex against their will. Most rape victims are women, but men can also be the victims of rape. Sexual assault covers any sort of sexual contact and behaviour that is unwanted. Rape is not always committed by a stranger to the victim; it can be committed by a family member or an acquaintance. When a victim is under 18, rape can often be referred to as child abuse. Sometimes a victim is given a drink spiked with a date-rape drug, which will make them unlikely to be able to resist such an assault.

Show your understanding

1 Why are rules and laws necessary to keep law and order in our society?
2 What is the role of the following in making laws for Scotland?
   - The Courts
   - The Scottish Parliament
   - The UK Parliament
3 What is criminal law?
4 What is civil law?
5 What is crime?
6 **(a)** Who decides what is a crime?
   (b) Give two examples of new crimes in Scotland.
7 Describe, in detail, the difference between blue-collar and white-collar crime.
8 Choose three different types of crime and find out about incidences of these crimes in your local area.

Crime statistics

Statistics about crime in Scotland can be found in the Scottish Crime and Justice Survey (SCJS) and in police recorded crime statistics. The SCJS asks the public about their experiences and perceptions of crime. This means that it is possible to compare and contrast two different sources of information on the scale and extent of crime in Scotland and on people's perceptions of crime. An important role of the SCJS is to provide an alternative and complementary measure of crime to the police recorded crime statistics, which provide statistics on crimes and offences recorded and cleared up by the eight Scottish police forces.

Crime statistics should be treated with care as they reflect reported crime. Not all crime is reported and some individuals for different reasons are reluctant to go to the police. They might have been assaulted but are too afraid to go to the police, or do not wish to report crimes committed by friends or neighbours, or might wish to take revenge in their own way.

WWW

Information about the Scottish Crime and Justice Survey can be found on the Scottish Government website: www.scotland.gov.uk/Topics/Statistics/Browse/Crime-Justice
Statistics can be found at: www.scotland.gov.uk/Topics/Statistics/Browse/Crime-Justice/Datasets

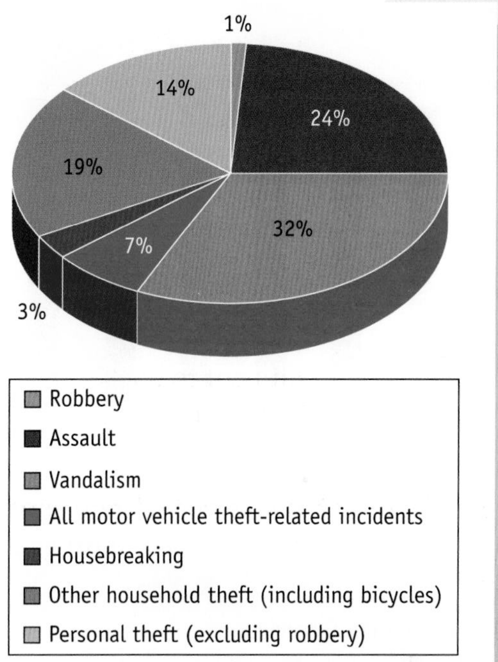

Source: Scottish Crime and Justice Survey 2010–11

Figure 1.6 Percentage of selected SCJS crime in each crime group

Results of the Scottish Crime and Justice Survey 2010–11

Figure 1.6 shows the percentage by crime group for all SCJS crime surveyed (not all crimes are surveyed).

Show your understanding

Branch out

1 Find out more about each of the crime categories in Figure 1.6 at www.scotland.gov.uk/Publications/2011/10/28142346/4

Violent crime statistics

Robbery and assault are described as violent crime. Vandalism, motor vehicle theft, housebreaking, household theft and personal theft are grouped together as property crime.

	2008–09	2010–11	% change
All SCJS crime	1,044,809	874,142	–16%
Robbery	19,967	12,027	–39%
Assault	296,893	208,109	–30%
Vandalism	350,376	275,387	–21%
All motor vehicle theft-related incidents	69,709	57,814	–17%
Housebreaking	25,485	28,144	10%
Other household theft (inc. bicycles)	172,856	169,110	–2%
Personal theft (excl. robbery)	109,793	123,551	13%

Source: Scottish Crime and Justice Survey 2010–11

Table 1.3 Percentage change in numbers of all SCJS crime by crime group

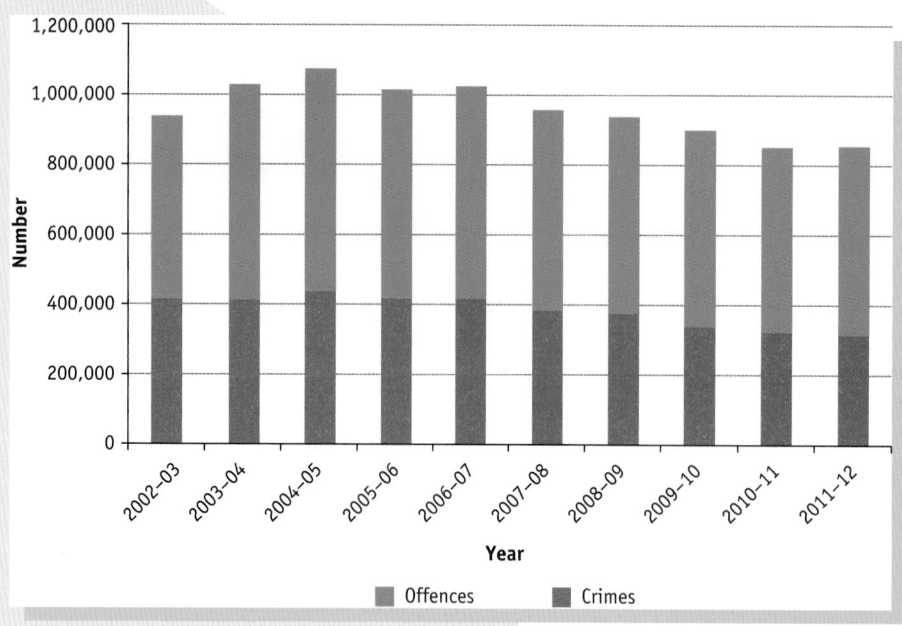

Source: Justice Analytical Services

Figure 1.7 Crimes and offences recorded by the police in Scotland 2002–12

Show your understanding

Develop your skills

1 'Vandalism has the highest crime category and there has been a reduction in all categories of all crime especially housebreaking.' *(Statement by crime researcher.)*
Using Figure 1.6 and Table 1.3, identify to what extent the crime researcher is being selective in the use of facts.

2 Using Figure 1.7, describe fully the trends of crime and offences recorded by the police from 2002–03 to 2011–12.

Branch out

3 Either on your own, as a group or as a class, access Scottish Government crime statistics using the link on page 13. Choose a category of crime.
Using the statistics, describe any pattern in the number of crimes committed over a period of time. Has the number of incidents of your chosen category increased, decreased, stayed the same or has the trend fluctuated? Compare your results with those of other members of your class.

Chapter 2

Causes and impact of crime

The causes of crime

What are the different causes of crime?

People are responsible for their own behaviour and accountable for their actions. However, societies need to provide the conditions for people to have the best possible chance of being able to act responsibly.

Often when explanations are given for why crime is committed, the reasons given are too simplistic. This can lead to stereotyping, prejudice and discrimination. Make sure you know the meaning of each of the words in Figure 2.1.

What you will learn:

1 The different causes of crime.
2 The main causes of crime.

Study Figure 2.1, which contains information about possible causes of crime. It is important to be able to link them in order to get a better understanding of this topic. There is an exercise at the end of this chapter that will help you to do this.

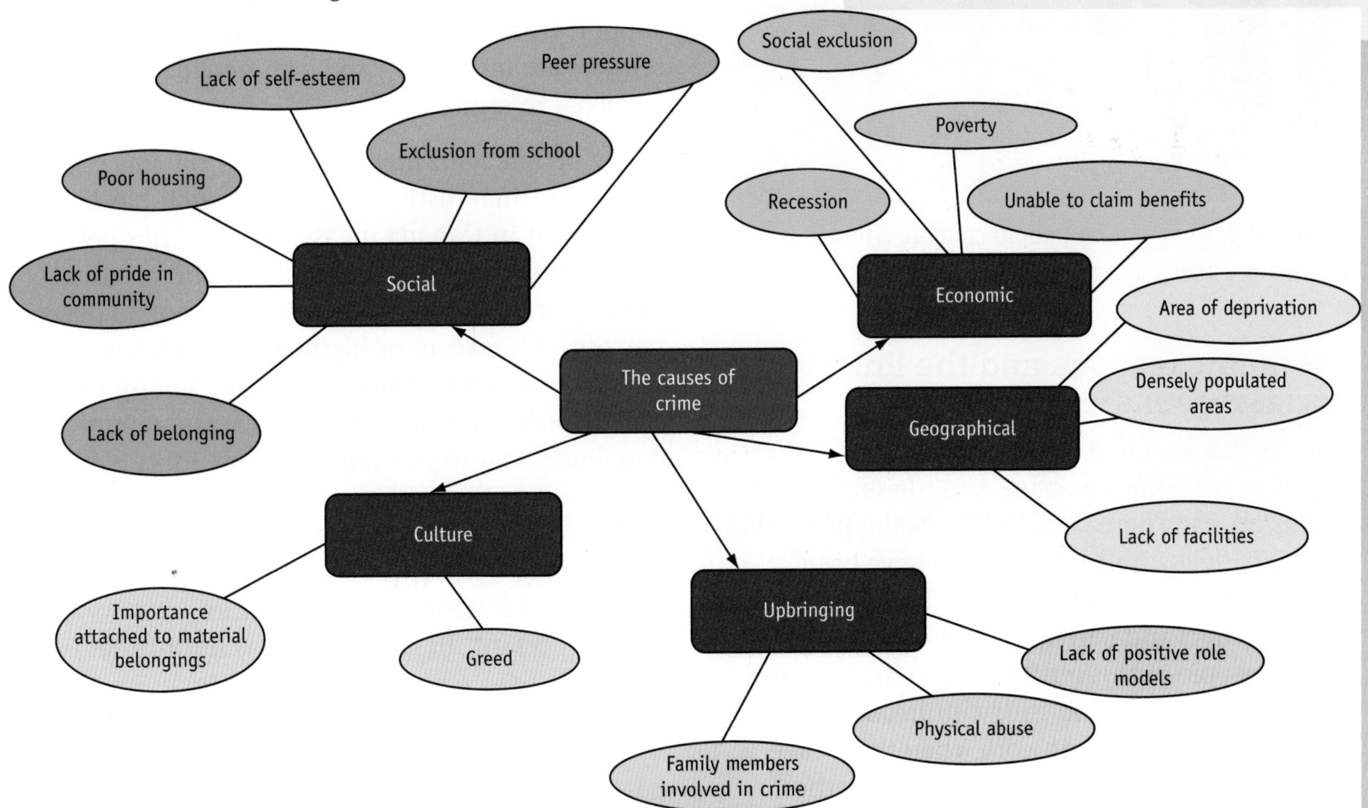

Figure 2.1 Possible causes of crime

Social reasons

When a young person or groups of young people commit crimes, there are usually social reasons. It can often be partly to do with some young people not having access to leisure facilities or not being able to take part in sports or other leisure activities due to poverty, and this leads to social exclusion. Young people from well-off families are more likely to be able to afford such leisure and sports activities. Some sports are very expensive, such as skiing and horse-riding. Public sporting facilities are often not as attractive as private clubs and this can put people off using them. Therefore young people from poorer socio-economic backgrounds may be more likely to get involved in criminal activity, either for material gain or for amusement and thrills.

Figure 2.2 When young people commit crimes, there are usually social reasons

Economic reasons and the links with social reasons

Poverty can lead to a lack of educational opportunities, poor housing and the social exclusion and stigma attached to being poor. Many young people who commit crime have been excluded from school. They may feel abandoned by their teachers and perhaps by their families too. Young people in this position often find comfort in belonging to gangs and gang culture. Some young people are unable to get work when they leave full-time education and cannot afford further education. Some are even denied benefits, for example Jobseeker's Allowance, and therefore have no money to give them a decent lifestyle. Because our society attaches so much importance to material belongings, it can lead some young people to commit crime to be able to acquire popular items such as electronic goods and fashionable clothes.

Long-term unemployment can cause a lack of self-esteem and frustration, especially in young males. Failure at school and insecure employment can combine to increase the risk of a person committing crime. Unemployed men who have served long-term prison sentences are more likely to reoffend.

There is not a direct link between poverty and crime. However, the conditions associated with crime can mean that people who live in poverty may be more susceptible to getting involved in crime. The social environment a young person is brought up in can influence their behaviour. Neglect, criminality in parents, parents arguing, inability to cope, family violence and abuse are all factors that can lead a child into crime. Children require good care and resources to be able to cope in today's modern world. Children who require support from social services and mental health services are more likely to be vulnerable to getting involved in crime.

Many people with mental health problems end up in the criminal justice system. Research has been carried out in Canada measuring the links between mental health, youth delinquency and criminal behaviour. It was found that the level of a young person's self-esteem or his/her ability to handle stress are linked to whether or not a young person will display delinquent behaviour. The report concludes that understanding these links is very important as this will encourage governments to develop policies for intervention and reduce reoffending. The report also found that experiences at home, at school and in the community were very important. In a survey it was found that 65% of youths who reported being highly involved with their school reported no aggression compared to 47% of those not involved. Also, 66% of youths who said they liked school reported no aggression compared with 47% who said they did not like school much.

Alcohol and drug abuse

FACT FILE

The British Crime Survey reported that:

'in nearly half (48%) of all violent incidents, victims believed offenders to be under the influence of alcohol. This figure rose to 60% in cases of "stranger violence".'

Alcohol abuse is linked most strongly to crimes of violence. Nearly half of all violent crimes are committed while the perpetrator is under the influence of alcohol. It has been found that 'frequency of drunkenness' was strongly linked to 'general offending and criminal and disorderly behaviour during and after drinking'.

However, research shows there is no single direct causal link between alcohol and violent or abusive behaviours; it is more of a complex mix of factors.

There are also indirect links to crime. Alcohol and drugs may create the sort of dysfunctional family from which children are more likely to turn to crime.

In 2007 the Scottish Government conducted a review of the law on alcohol-related crime. The intention of this review was to make clear to offenders that alcohol will not be seen as a mitigating factor in criminal activity. The Justice Secretary Kenny MacAskill said, 'We in Scotland have a cultural problem with alcohol. Too many Scots think it acceptable to get drunk. Abused partners, random assaults, stabbings and vandalism – the impact is there for all to see – on the streets, in the police stations, in hospital emergency departments, and in the courts.' (See page 32.)

The most recent statistics show that 7 out of 10 of those accused of murder in Scotland had been drinking or on drugs. Nearly half of Scotland's 7,000 prisoners say they were drunk at the time they committed their offence.

The Justice Secretary continued: 'The Scottish Government is developing a long-term strategic

Figure 2.3 Alcohol abuse is strongly linked to crimes of violence

approach to shifting attitudes and changing behaviour towards alcoholism. The misuse of alcohol does much more harm to our society than violence and crime alone – it is a significant factor holding back the health of the nation.'

There is much evidence to support the idea that those with a drug use dependency are more likely to be arrested for crimes such as burglary or shop theft, or for robbery and handling stolen goods: crimes that will help to pay for their drug habit.

However, the question of whether drug use leads people into criminal activity or whether those who use drugs are already predisposed to such activity is debatable.

Location and crime

Evidence shows that criminal activity is not evenly distributed geographically. Some areas suffer higher crime rates than others. These areas are sometimes called 'hot spots'. The economic status or wealth of an area is an important factor. Studies have found that robberies are higher than the average in poorer areas with higher levels of social problems. The highest rates of violent crime also occur in the poorer areas.

However, social and economic inequality might have a greater effect than poverty alone. Poverty might have a greater effect on crime in urban rather than in rural areas. Taking inequality into account, studies have shown that urban areas tend to be more mixed than rural areas and therefore have higher levels of inequality.

There may also be more victims of crime in disadvantaged areas. Some studies have found that demand for police services is higher in more disadvantaged areas. Victims in disadvantaged areas are more likely to suffer crime closer to their own homes and a repeated number of times in their own neighbourhood. It has also been found that people in disadvantaged areas may be the target of crime because they are more likely to carry cash.

Areas that suffer higher rates of long-term unemployment are also likely to suffer more crime. Young people not in school and unemployed may be more likely to get involved in crime. The lack of provision of suitable apprenticeships for young people is a contributory factor. Densely populated cities with large populations and concentrations of drug users will also produce higher crime rates and victim rates. However, crimes may not be reported if the victim is a drug user.

Figure 2.4 Crime is most likely to occur in poorer areas

Gender and crime

There are differences between men and women in terms of their criminal behaviour and their experiences of the criminal justice system. By far the majority of crime in Scotland is committed by men, and when women offend they tend to commit low-level, non-violent offences and pose little risk to society. In 2008–09 women constituted only 15% of all convictions in Scotland and they form a mere 5% of the prison population in Scotland.

Show your understanding

1 Copy Figure 2.1 on page 15. Can you add any more causes of crime?
2 On the diagram you have drawn, make as many connections as you can between the different factors. Discuss the connections in groups.
3 Read the following statement:
'People are responsible for their own behaviour and have only themselves to blame if they get involved in criminal activities.'
Explain why some might agree with the statement and why some would disagree with it. In your conclusion, mention whether you agree or disagree with the statement.
4 Does drug use lead people into criminal activity or are those who use drugs already predisposed to such activity? Discuss.

Branch out

5 'Social and economic inequality might have a greater effect than poverty alone.' Consider why this could be true.

Case study: Causes of the 2011 riots in England

Opinion differs on the causes of the 2011 riots which began in the London boroughs and spread to Manchester, Birmingham, Bristol and Liverpool. A *Guardian* article stated that the riots represented 'the most serious bout of civil unrest in a generation'. Five people died and more than 2,500 shops and businesses were damaged. More than 2,000 participants in the riots were arrested and 1,400 sent to jail.

The situation began on 4 August 2011 when Mark Duggan, a 29-year-old black man from Tottenham, was shot and killed by police. He was suspected of being in possession of a hand gun. Mark's death led to a public protest in Tottenham over the circumstances of his killing. It was a peaceful protest but later that night violence broke out, and so began the riots. Some argue that this event sparked off the riots, but the events that followed were not race riots.

Reading the Riots is a joint study by the *Guardian* and the London School of Economics (LSE) into the causes of the 2011 riots. Professor Tim Newburn, a former adviser to the Metropolitan Police and Home Office, Head of LSE's Social Policy Department, said, 'There is an urgent need for some rigorous social research which will look, without prejudice, at the causes and the consequences of the recent riots.' He felt that it was very important to speak with those involved in the riots, including the police and victims. In interviews with the rioters, 85% of those questioned said policing was an 'important' or 'very important' factor in why the riots happened.

Here are some of the responses given by the rioters:

- 'The police is the biggest gang out there.'
- 'Abuse of police power in their communities.'
- 'They just generally class you as someone that's bad like that.'

Figure 2.5 A scene from the riots in England in 2011

- In response to the question 'Do the police in your area do a good or bad job?' only 7% of *Reading the Riots* respondents said 'excellent' or 'good', compared to 56% of respondents to the same question in the British Crime Survey.
- 73% said they had been stopped and searched in the past 12 months; they were more than eight times more likely than the general population in London to have been stopped and searched in the previous year.

In an ICM poll, while rioters cited poverty and policing as the two most important causes of the riots, when the general population was surveyed, poor parenting (86%) and criminality (86%) were said to be the leading riot causes. One newspaper columnist blamed 'feral parents [who were] too drunk or drugged or otherwise out of it' to care if their children were out looting and burning.

Gender and the riots

Government data has estimated that only 10% of those who took part in the riots were female. But from the *Reading the Riots* research, girls and women appear to have played a significant role in the disorder. In the study, interviews carried out with female rioters revealed complex reasons for their involvement. Similar to the men who rioted,

some were there only to loot and exploit the anarchic situation; others said that they had no intention of stealing and that they got caught up in the moment.

Social networking and the spread of the riots

During and immediately after the riots, many media reports claimed that social media played an important part in inciting, organising and spreading the riots. Some politicians and commentators called for Twitter to be closed down, but studies have shown that there is no significant evidence of Twitter playing such a part. In fact, it was found that Twitter proved valuable in mobilising support among people who volunteered to clean up.

On the other hand it was suggested that free mobile phone messaging provided a fast and free method of communication and seems to have been used by many who took part in the riots.

Poverty and the riots

Home Office research found that those appearing at court tended to be from more deprived circumstances than the wider population of England:

- 35% of adults were claiming out-of-work benefits (compared to 12% of the working age population).
- 42% of young people brought before the courts had free school meals, only available in England to the 16% of secondary school pupils from the poorest backgrounds.
- 58% of those appearing in court identified their residential location as being within the 20% most deprived areas in England – which matches what the Home Office found.
- 46% were black mixed race and 42% were white.
- 75% had a previous conviction and 90% were male.

The police point of view

Officers interviewed as part of the study said further disorder was likely, with many citing worsening social and economic conditions as the potential cause.

Figure 2.6 David Cameron

David Cameron's view

'These riots were not about poverty. That insults the millions of people who, whatever the hardship, would never dream of making others suffer like this … [it comes down to] a lack of proper parenting, a lack of proper upbringing, a lack of proper ethics, a lack of proper morals.'

WERE THE RIOTS ABOUT RACE?

If anything, the ethnic mix said something about the way various communities coexist in the capital. One young black man who joined the melee in Tottenham described what he saw. 'Originally it started off, it was like, yes it was a group of black people … but I seen Hasidic Jews from Stamford Hill who were down there. I seen lots of white people. I seen guys from shops – Turkish, it turned out. It was like the whole neighbourhood came out. The neighbourhood knew it was all wrong. But sadly it was the neighbourhood that got trashed. They were all out in support.' Another was also struck by the diversity. 'I can't even count the numbers, yeah, of different ethnicities that I saw there,' he said.

The police came under attack. Shops and offices and stores came under attack. But they appear to have been targeted as symbols of the establishment rather than as part of any kind of racial statement.

Extract from a *Guardian* article, 8 December 2011

Show your understanding

1 Read the case study on the riots in England in 2011. List the causes of the riots.

2 'Crime is caused by poverty and social exclusion.' Discuss. Write an extended exam-style answer to this statement.

Develop your skills

3 Write a report on the causes of the riots. Include in your report:
- Introduction and summary of what happened.
- The opinions of the rioters.
- The opinion of the general public.
- Profiles of those who were convicted.
- Conclusion with your opinion of the main cause(s).

The impact of crime

What you will learn:

1 The impact of crime on the victim and on the offender.

2 The economic impact of crime on the community.

3 The social/emotional impact of crime on the community.

How does crime affect local communities?

The following case studies will give you an idea of how crime affects victims and local communities.

Case study: The impact of crime on the victim

On Friday night Anna, a young nursing student, was robbed coming home from a shift in a hospital. Although she wasn't hurt in any way, she was terrified out of her wits. Her phone, passport, purse and hospital ID were all taken. This led to the hassle of contacting the police, cancelling cards and contacting the passport office and phone provider. But more serious is the fact that Anna is now terrified to make her way home from work in the evenings and is having to rely on lifts and taxis.

Anna says that she feels so nervous she is wary of anyone walking in the hospital grounds after dark and is startled by the slightest sound. Anna says that the experience has dented her confidence and is taking her mind off her work and her studies.

Source: www.thestudentroom.co.uk/

Case study: Distraction burglary

Distraction burglary occurs when one person 'distracts' the victim, then another person commits a crime, such as robbery. This could happen, for example, by ringing the front door bell and engaging the victim in conversation. While this is going on, a second person will enter the property by another means and perform the robbery.

Prevention advice on this crime type is available on the Crimestoppers website. On the website, Lord Ashcroft, KCMG, Founder and Chair of Crimestoppers, said, 'Distraction burglars are clearly hideous individuals as they tend to prey on elderly, vulnerable people to rob them of life-long treasured possessions by using devious tactics and, in many cases, violence. Some victims suffer a decline in health and even die as a result of the trauma caused by these criminals. If you have any information on these wanted individuals, please contact the charity Crimestoppers anonymously, we guarantee that no one will know your identity.'

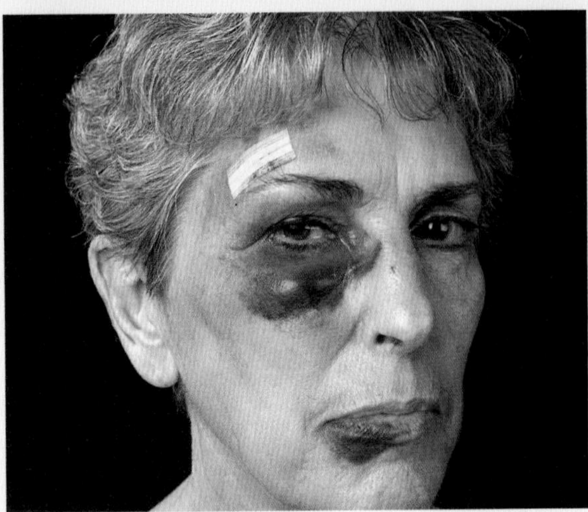

Figure 2.7 Distraction burglars often target the elderly and use violence

Dame Vera Lynn, co-patron of Sussex Crimestoppers branch, said, 'As someone who has been a victim of burglary several times, I can't reinforce enough how frightening it is. Worse than having your possessions taken, is having your confidence stolen as well.'

Source: www.crimestoppers-uk.org/media-centre/news-releases/2010/most-wanted-distraction-burglars-target-the-elderly

Case study: The impact of crime on the offender

The young people who got caught up in the 2011 riots didn't think about the consequences of their actions. For example, a 21-year-old who stole a case of bottled water is now serving six months in prison. This will have a negative impact on his ability to lead as full a life as he would wish when he is released. The majority of employers will ask about previous convictions. He also lost his job because he was jailed. He had thought that in the future he would like to go into teaching but his criminal conviction would now show up with the disclosure process. He could find it difficult to get a visa if he wanted to visit certain countries such as the USA. It could also be difficult to get a mortgage. The prime minister has backed plans for people who 'loot and pillage their own community' to be evicted from council houses.

Case study: The economic impact of crime

The cost of crime has an impact on individuals, taxpayers and the government.

During the riot in 2011, the windows of businesses were smashed and stock was looted. Many business owners lost thousands of pounds worth of stock. Vehicles were set on fire and road signs were damaged. All of this costs the taxpayer money to put right and it also puts insurance premiums up, making it more expensive for people to run their businesses and possibly leading to more job losses. There were nearly 5,000 compensation claims following the riots.

Case study: The emotional impact of crime

Many people feel less confident about their communities and running their businesses if they have witnessed or been a victim of crime. The emotional impact on victims of crime often leads to the need for mental health services, to provide support for the trauma caused by the criminal act.

IMPACT ON THE WIDER COMMUNITY

Letting Our Communities Flourish – A Strategy for Tackling Serious Organised Crime in Scotland

In the introduction to this report, Kenny MacAskill writes:

'Serious organised crime causes devastating harm to our communities. Members of organised crime groups are ruthless and selfish. They do not care about the misery they bring to people's lives through violence, crime and addiction – often to those who live in our hardest hit communities. Every community is affected, and the problem is global. Drugs and prostitution affect every area of Scotland. There were 455 drug-related deaths in 2007 – the highest ever – and the social and economic costs of drug misuse are estimated to be over £2.6 billion a year. Fraud and counterfeiting drive up prices and insurance costs for hard-pressed families, and help to fund other activities like illegal firearms trading, violence and drug dealing. The cost of fraud to every man, woman and child in Scotland is estimated to be £330 per year, and much of this fraud is carried out by serious organised crime groups. Serious organised criminals make money at the expense of hardworking, law abiding people, undermining legitimate businesses, potentially distorting democracy and threatening the fabric of our communities.

Source: Scottish Government

Racially motivated crime

Despite the fact that laws have been passed to tackle racism and racially motivated crime, racism is still a problem across Scotland and the United Kingdom. Racism can take many forms. No matter what form it takes it impacts negatively on the lives and livelihoods of many people in our communities. Racism divides communities and creates antagonism and resentment among people of different ethnic groups and cultures. Education programmes, such as Show Racism the Red Card, are very effective at highlighting the negative aspects of racist attitudes and behaviour and teaching people about the best way to tackle racism.

FACT FILE

Scottish Household Survey (2006)

According to the Scottish Household Survey (2006), aspects of the neighbourhood most disliked among those living in the 15% most deprived areas include no sense of community, problem residents and substance abuse. For the remainder of the population, these aspects were also significantly important, though living in an unpleasant environment was, for this large group, the main aspect of neighbourhood that was particularly disliked. Living in a safe environment was an aspect of neighbourhood particularly liked by all respondents, but especially those who did not live in the 15% most deprived areas.

Source: Scottish Government

WWW

Pupils can find out more about the impact of crime in the community at the following websites:

www.aboutequalopportunities.co.uk/fighting-racism-community.html

www.scotland.gov.uk/Resource/Doc/274127/0081989.pdf

Show your understanding

1 Draw a spider diagram to show the different ways in which crime impacts on local communities.

Branch out

2 Add to your spider diagram to show other ways in which crime can impact on local communities. Look at local newspapers to get ideas of how people in your local area have been affected. You could find out if your local councillor/MSP/MP is asked to deal with problems associated with crime on behalf of their constituents. Ask your campus cop, if you have one.

Chapter 3

Efforts to tackle crime

Policing in Scotland

The role of the police

The main role of the police is to:

- maintain law and order
- detect criminals
- prevent crime
- protect the public.

What you will learn:

1 The role of the police.
2 The structure of the new Scottish Police Service.
3 Arguments for and against a single police force.
4 Styles of policing and crime prevention.

The Scottish Parliament is responsible for most of the powers and functions of the police in Scotland. This means that most aspects of policing are devolved to the Scottish Parliament. However, the UK Government retains responsibility for passing laws on terrorism, security, firearms and drugs. The police have a duty to uphold and enforce the law and maintain the peace in Scotland.

Police reform

The process of police reform began in the summer of 2012 when legislation setting out Scottish Government plans for a single Police Service for Scotland was approved by the Scottish Parliament.

The Scottish Government stated that a single Police Service will protect and improve frontline services amid severe budget reductions from the Westminster Government. It aims to provide a more equal service across Scotland and provide clearer national governance of police services.

The new Scottish Police Service is a merger of the eight Scottish police forces (see Figure 3.1). It also includes the Scottish Crime and Drug Enforcement Agency, the Scottish Police Services Authority and the Scottish Police College.

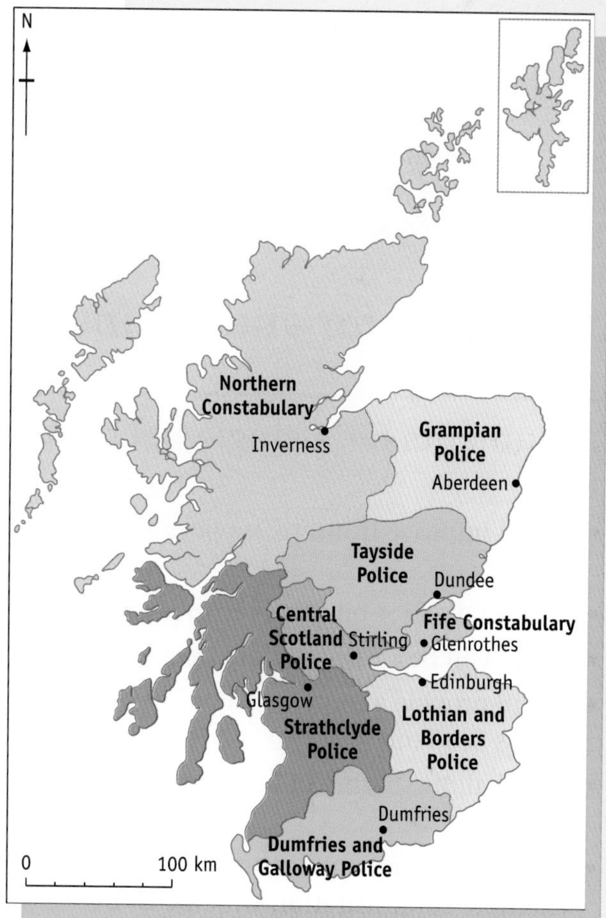

Figure 3.1 The old Scottish police authorities

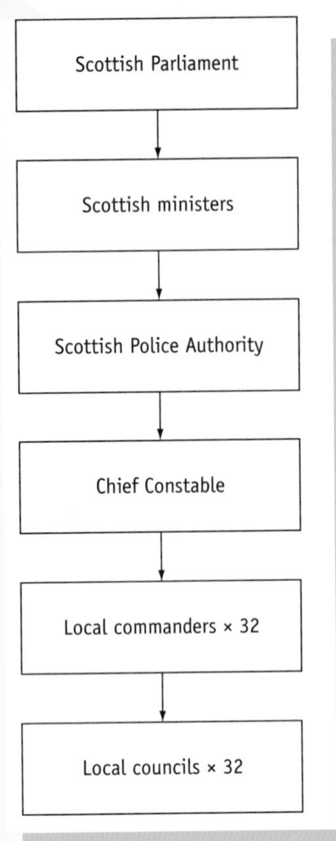

Figure 3.2 The structure of the new Scottish Police Service

Concern had been expressed about how local frontline services would be maintained but the new police authority which came into force on 1 April 2013 has appointed local senior officers to each council area with a duty to work with local councils to shape services that meet the needs of local communities.

In September 2012, Chief Constable Stephen House of Strathclyde Police was announced as the first Chief Constable of the new Police Service of Scotland. He was sworn in to the post on 1 October 2012.

Figure 3.3 Scottish police controlling a protest

Arguments for and against a single police force

Arguments for a single police force

- It will improve frontline services amid budget cuts.
- It will save £1.4 billion over 15 years.
- There will be clearer national governance.
- It will provide a more equal police service across Scotland.
- It will allow sharing of ideas and policies.
- It will eliminate duplication of services, for example administration which cost £40 million a year under the old eight police force system.

Arguments against a single police force

- There are concerns about who will be in charge of frontline services in local areas.
- Different areas have different needs, e.g. urban areas compared with rural areas.
- The eight forces had a 'good understanding' of local needs and had boosted community policing. The single force may not be able to keep up with the changing needs of different local areas.
- The lack of accountability of the Chief Constable could be a problem.
- A possible reduction in the number of police officers might lead to problems in tackling crime on the frontline.

Different styles of policing

Community policing

While community policing is about the way policing is carried out in our communities, the Scottish Government stresses that it is about partnership between different groups such as the police, local authorities, social work, education and individuals, emphasising the responsibility of local citizens. Community policing is very important in helping the Scottish Government to achieve the aims of helping the public to feel safer and have more confidence in the police and in reducing crime.

Section 10 of *The Scottish Community Policing Engagement Principles* states that community policing involves officers:

- ★ being visible, accessible, present and readily identifiable in the community and discrete when that is appropriate
- ★ communicating as widely as possible using all appropriate means
- ★ consulting, listening and responding
- ★ recognising individual needs and prioritising support to those groups of people most vulnerable to harm
- ★ working closely with other public and voluntary services and businesses to encourage people to take responsibility for their actions and how they affect others
- ★ being involved in a problem-solving approach to local crime issues and accountable to communities for local policing
- ★ working in partnership with other public and voluntary services and businesses on the ground to make people feel safer.

Source: *The Scottish Community Policing Engagement Principles*, Scottish Government

Case study: Taser guns

Figure 3.4 Police are trained to use taser guns

Taser guns use 50,000 volts of electricity to stop criminals without injuring them permanently.

Opinion differs on their use.

A day in the life of a police officer often involves dealing with violence and sometimes armed criminals. Police can disarm criminals using taser guns from a greater distance than without them, making it safer for the police and other members of the community. Taser guns are unlikely to kill, but they can kill. Some taser guns have cameras on them to record the situation to try to make sure they are used properly.

Tasers in Scotland

As firearms policy is now devolved to the Scottish Parliament, chief constables in Scotland have to have authorisation to implement the use of taser guns. This authorisation would be needed if the pilot scheme introduced in 2011 was to be rolled out more widely across Scotland.

Amnesty International has branded a six-month taser gun pilot scheme in Scotland 'unlawful'. John Watson, Scottish programme

director for Amnesty International, said: 'The Firearms Act clearly states that new police deployments of taser must have written authorisation from Government ministers.' Amnesty say tasers 'have a role' in policing but should be handled by properly trained people acting on decisions by senior officers.

In the USA 500 men have died after being tasered; most were unarmed. Two men in England were killed by tasers in 2011.

There are arguments for and against police carrying taser guns, as the following articles show.

POLICE OFFICER STABBED

A police constable in the Metropolitan Police who was stabbed with a ten-inch butcher's knife while on duty in London required extensive surgery. The attack led to the Metropolitan Police Commissioner calling for police response officers to be armed routinely with taser guns.

The officer who was attacked was asked if a taser would have helped him. PC Harding said from what he had seen, he thought it could have made a difference. 'The taser is a valuable tool. It's been proven to work,' he added.

Source: BBC News, London, 10 December 2012

BLIND MAN TASERED BY THE POLICE

In 2012 a police officer who was looking for a man carrying a Samurai sword mistakenly shot a blind man, Colin Farmer, with a taser gun. The 63 year old collapsed in shock and was hand-cuffed. The innocent man was taken to hospital for treatment and later discharged.

He said he was now scared to go outside. Some argue that this adds to the arguments against taser guns – that innocent citizens can be harmed.

Show your understanding

Branch out

1 Do you think the police should be allowed to carry taser guns?

2 Consider the following:
 (a) Is the use of taser guns inevitable considering the rise in gun and knife crime?
 (b) Will it lead to police abusing their powers?

ICT task

Find out about the arguments for and against an armed police force.

Crime prevention – who is responsible?

Crime prevention is everyone's responsibility. This is reflected in the Scottish Government's framework for tackling antisocial behaviour. In March 2009, the Scottish Government and the Convention of Scottish Local Authorities (COSLA) jointly published their framework for tackling antisocial behaviour, 'Promoting Positive Outcomes'. The framework is structured around 'four pillars': prevention; integration; engagement and communication.

Emphasis is placed on addressing the causes of antisocial behaviour such as drink, drugs and deprivation. The framework advocates promoting positive behaviour through the use of role models and mentors as well as punishing bad behaviour. By creating more choices and more chances for people to succeed, the chances of them being involved in antisocial behaviour will be reduced.

It is suggested that this will work best by services such as social work, education and police working together.

The National Crime Squad

The National Crime Squad (NCS) deals with serious organised crime in the UK, therefore adopting a co-ordinated national approach. The types of crimes the NCS deal with include kidnap, extortion, international drug trafficking, arms smuggling, people smuggling and money laundering among others.

Figure 3.5 Armed police patrolling at a UK airport

Counter-terrorism

While counter-terrorism policy and legislation is reserved to the Westminster Government, certain aspects of preparation, prevention and dealing with the consequences of a terrorist act in Scotland would be managed and controlled by the Scottish Government and local agencies.

The Scottish Government is engaged in a range of activities to address the threat, which integrate with the UK Government's overarching 'CONTEST' counter-terrorism strategy.

CONTEST

CONTEST is the UK Government's strategy for countering terrorism. It is made up of four main strands:

- Pursue – the pursuit of terrorists and those that sponsor them
- Prevent – disrupting terrorist activities and countering those factors which push and pull people into violent extremism and terrorism
- Protect – protecting the public and national interests and making the UK a harder target through better protective security
- Prepare – to reduce and ultimately minimise the potential harm caused by terrorist attacks... [and] to improve our resilience to cope with attacks.

Source: Scottish Government

Tackling and preventing knife crime

The SNP government has made tackling knife crime a major priority – in 2010, 35 people were killed by a sharp instrument. High profile coverage of, for example, the murder of 19-year-old Reamonn Gormley in 2011 has made knife crime a major issue of public concern. Reamonn's murder in his home town of Blantyre shocked the community and led to 1,000 people marching through the streets of Blantyre to honour Reamonn and to demand further action.

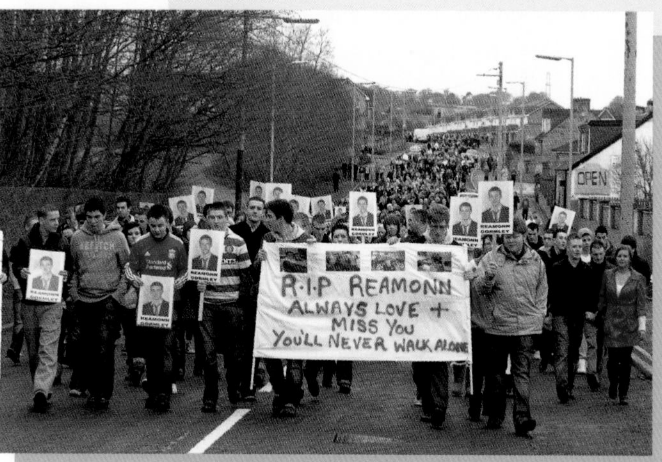

Figure 3.6 Around 1,000 people marched through Blantyre to honor Reamonn Gormley and to demand action against knife crime

The SNP government would argue that there has been a record increase in stop-and-search across Scotland, supported by education, through initiatives such as the *No knives, better lives* campaign (see following page). Courts have been given powers to impose four-year sentences for carrying a knife. Since 2007 there has been a 30% decrease in offensive weapons crime.

The following message about the danger of carrying knives appears on the Police Scotland website.

Knife crime

You can help protect yourself and others from knife crime by making wise choices.

Don't carry a knife

Even if you don't intend to use it, you are putting yourself at risk. You are also putting yourself in a position where you could kill someone. A single stab wound can be fatal.

Never look after a knife for someone else

Most knife incidents in the West of Scotland involve young men between the ages of 16 and 25. Sometimes, a teenage girl will carry a knife in her handbag for her boyfriend in the belief that she won't be searched. Police can and do use hand-held metal detectors to seek out hidden weapons. **If you carry a knife, chances are you will be caught.**

Keep school safe and blade-free

Knife possession and knife crime are rare in Scottish schools. However, if you know of someone who brings a knife to school, it is important that you tell someone.

Report your worries to a teacher, or telephone Crimestoppers on 0800 555 111, where you can pass the information on anonymously.

Source: Police Scotland

Show your understanding

1 Who is responsible for the powers and functions of the police in Scotland?
2 Outline the role of the police in Scotland.
3 Describe what reform has taken place in policing.
4 Draw a diagram showing the structure of the Scottish Police Service.
5 Describe the following, in detail:
   (a) Community policing.
   (b) Counter-terrorism measures in Scotland.
   (c) The work of the National Crime Squad.
   (d) Strategies to prevent knife crime.

The laws on alcohol and drugs

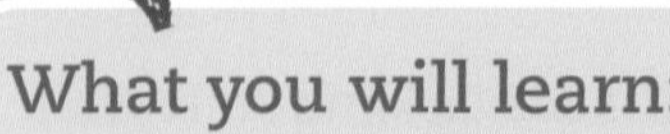

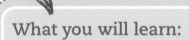

What you will learn:

1 The laws regarding alcohol, drugs and road traffic offences.
2 How successful these laws are.

Scotland's alcohol problem

Alcohol is a legal drug, but misuse can lead to health problems and disorderliness. It is stated on the Scottish Government website that 'It is becoming increasingly evident that as a nation our relationship with alcohol has become unbalanced' and that 'In 2010, 23% more alcohol was sold per adult in Scotland than in England and Wales, the widest gap to date.' It is for these reasons that new legislation has been introduced to help tackle this problem.

Laws regarding alcohol

Scottish laws on alcohol are a mixture of Scottish laws and those that apply across the UK. There are a number of laws governing its sale, purchase and consumption. Recent legislation passed in the Scottish Parliament aims to address the problems caused by alcohol and drugs.

Alcohol (Minimum Pricing) (Scotland) Act 2012

This Act states that alcohol must not be sold on the premises at a price below its minimum price. The Act introduces a 50p minimum price per unit and this will lead to higher prices. The intention is that higher prices will lead to reduced consumption. Both the police and health authorities support this law. However, critics argue that this move will only increase the profits of supermarkets and that some cheap and popular drinks such as fortified tonic wine will not see a price rise.

Alcohol age limits

- People who are 18 years of age or older can buy alcohol. However, the licence holder can refuse to allow anyone under 21 on the premises if they wish.
- People over the age of 16 can buy beer, wine or cider as long as it is served with a meal and consumed in an area used solely for eating meals. It is illegal for people under the age of 18 to buy or be sold alcohol in any other circumstances.
- Children who are 14 or over are allowed on licensed premises but can't buy alcohol or have it bought for them.
- From 2009, Scotland's law has been that buying alcohol for anyone under 18 is an offence punishable by a fine up to £5,000 and/or a prison sentence of up to three months.

FACT FILE

Alcohol misuse in Scotland

- There were more than 40,000 hospital admittances in 2007–08 due to alcohol-related illness and injury.
- Alcohol-related mortality has more than doubled in the last 15 years.
- Scotland has one of the fastest growing rates of liver disease and cirrhosis in the world.
- Excessive drinking can cause families to break down.
- It can result in crime and disorder.
- There is a link between the rise in the Scots murder rate (rose by 19% between 2010 and 2011) and alcohol.
- More than three-quarters of murders were committed under the influence of alcohol in 2011.
- Alcohol causes loss of productivity through sickness. It is estimated that alcohol misuse costs Scotland £2.25 billion every year.
- Up to 50% of men and up to 30% of women across Scotland exceed recommended weekly guidelines.

Source: Scottish Government

Laws regarding driving and alcohol

Road Safety Scotland is very much concerned with the safety of all road users and it warns about the effects and consequences of drink driving. Getting rid of the effects of alcohol from the body is a very slow process that takes hours rather than minutes. There is no way of speeding up alcohol elimination. A person can still be over the legal limit the morning after an evening's drinking.

In November 2012, plans to cut the drink-driving limit in Scotland were endorsed by the Scottish Parliament. The SNP government proposed reducing the limit from 80 milligrams per 100ml of blood to 50 milligrams. This action was in response to Westminister's decision to grant more powers to the Scottish Parliament including setting the legal alcohol limit for driving.

Public drunkenness and nuisance behaviour

It is an offence to be drunk in a public place, even though most people won't have to appear in court because of it. The Criminal Justice (Scotland) Act 1980 designated places where the police can take drunk and incapable people to sober up.

POLICE SOS BUS IN GLASGOW TO HELP DRUNKEN REVELLERS

An emergency bus staffed by Red Cross volunteers is being laid on in Glasgow city centre over the festive period to help drunk or injured revellers. The SOS bus will treat people who have consumed too much alcohol. The SOS bus also helps assault victims, people in emotional distress and those fleeing from domestic abuse.

It will be parked outside Glasgow Central Station in Gordon Street between 22:00 and 04:00 every Friday and Saturday over the festive period.

The service is launched for what is traditionally the busiest weekend in Glasgow for Christmas parties.

Source: www.bbc.co.uk/news

'Alcohol: A Framework for Action' Report

Harry Burns, Scotland's Chief Medical Officer, stated in the introduction to this 2012 report by the Scottish Government, 'There is no doubt that alcohol misuse claims many hundreds of lives in Scotland every year – twice as many today as 15 years ago – and that it hits our poorest communities the hardest. It has become a major health, economic and social challenge for our people, a problem which is damaging families and communities across the country. We have a responsibility to do all we can to tackle it. In Scotland, we led the way on smoking and we can lead the way on alcohol misuse too. Every one of us must ask, frankly, whether we are part of the problem and whether we are going to be part of the solution.'

Figure 3.7 Scotland's Chief Medical Officer, Harry Burns

Consequences of drink driving

Nearly one in seven of all deaths on Scottish roads involves drivers who are over the legal drink-drive limit. The risk of being involved in an accident increases rapidly with the amount of alcohol consumed.

Causing death by careless driving while under the influence of drink or drugs will result in a maximum 14-year jail sentence and a minimum two-year driving ban.

Driving or attempting to drive while above the legal limit or failing to provide a specimen will result in a maximum six-month jail sentence and a fine of £5,000 plus at least a 12-month disqualification.

Other consequences of a drink-drive conviction include a minimum 20-year criminal record, possible loss of livelihood, increased insurance costs, extreme difficulty in hiring a car and travelling to certain countries (e.g. USA), hefty legal expenses and social stigma.

In Scotland, being caught a second time can also result in you losing possession of your car. Cars forfeited under this scheme will be sold or destroyed.

The laws regarding illegal drugs

The Misuse of Drugs Act 1971

It is an arrestable offence for any person:

- ★ to import or export a controlled drug
- ★ to produce a controlled drug
- ★ to supply or offer to supply a controlled drug to another

It is an offence for any person:

- ★ to have a controlled drug in their possession (if possession is of a Class C drug then proceeding should be by way of a summons)
- ★ to have a controlled drug in their possession, whether lawful or not, with intent to supply it to another
- ★ to cultivate any plant of the genus *Cannabis*
- ★ being the occupier or concerned in the management of any premises, to knowingly permit or suffer any:
  - ★ production or attempted production of a controlled drug
  - ★ supply, attempt to supply or offer to supply, a controlled drug
  - ★ smoking of cannabis, cannabis resin or prepared opium
  - ★ smoking or other use of prepared opium.

Figure 3.8 The aftermath of a road traffic accident

Dangerous and careless driving/riding

The Road Traffic Act 1988

It is an arrestable offence for a person:

- ★ to cause the death of another person by driving a mechanically propelled vehicle dangerously on a road or any other public place
- ★ to drive a mechanically propelled vehicle on a road or any other public place:
  - ★ without due care and attention, or
  - ★ without reasonable consideration for other persons using the road or public place
- ★ to ride a cycle on a road without due care and attention, or without reasonable consideration for other persons using the road
- ★ to refuse to give name and address or give a false name and address.

The remaining offences are normally by way of summons.

- ★ A person driving a mechanically propelled vehicle on a road must stop the vehicle if asked to do so by a constable in uniform (Section 163, Road Traffic Act 1988).
- ★ A person driving a motor vehicle on a road or who a constable has reasonable cause to believe has committed an offence in relation to the use of that motor vehicle on a road must, on being required by a constable, produce his licence so as to enable the constable to ascertain the name and address of the holder.
- ★ A person required by a constable to produce his licence must, on being so required by the constable, state his date of birth.

Scotland's Road Safety Framework 2020 targets

Scotland's Road Safety Framework was launched in June 2009. It set out the vision for road safety in Scotland, the main priorities and issues, and included Scotland-specific targets and milestones which have been adopted from 2010.

Category	2015 milestone % reduction	2020 target % reduction
People killed	30	40
People seriously injured	43	55
Children (aged <16) killed	35	50
Children (aged <16) seriously injured	50	65

Source: *Scotland's Road Safety Framework to 2020*, Scottish Government

Table 3.1 Scotland's road safety milestones

How successful are the laws on alcohol, drink driving and drug offences?

	Fatal	Serious	Slight injury
1970	758	7,860	13,515
1985	550	6,507	13,587
1995	361	4,071	12,102
2000	297	3,007	11,828
2005	264	2,252	10,922
2010	189	1,712	8,394
2011	176	1,669	8,124

(This table represents accidents not casualties; more than one casualty could be involved in each accident.)

Source: Scottish Transport Statistics

Table 3.2 Road accidents by severity, 1970–2011

	2001	2005	2008	2011	% change 2008–2011
Built-up roads					
Fatal	91	76	82	62	–24%
Serious	1,557	1,224	1,277	951	–26%
Slight injury	7,788	7,087	6,104	5,341	–12.5%
Non-built-up roads					
Fatal	218	188	163	114	–24%
Serious	1,283	1,028	965	720	–25%
Slight injury	3,787	3,835	3,567	2,786	–22%

Source: Scottish Transport Statistics

Table 3.3 Reported accidents by type of road and severity

	2002–03	2004–05	2005–06	2007–08	2009–10	2011–12
Driving with excess blood alcohol	7,892	7,465	7,337	7,177	5,840	4,889
Speeding in restricted areas	66,422	123,926	93,495	65,420	50,788	53,068
Seatbelt offences	31,012	29,653	27,308	26,917	30,280	32,721

Source: Scottish Transport Statistics

Table 3.4 Motor vehicle offences recorded by the police by type of offence

Good news

- Accidents involving drink driving have decreased hugely over the last 30 years.
- Deaths and serious injuries related to drink driving have fallen by more than three-quarters since 1980.

Bad news

- Traffic accidents are still a leading cause of alcohol-related deaths among young men aged 16 to 24.
- In 2010, nearly 10,000 reported road casualties happened when a driver was over the legal alcohol limit. This represents 5% of all road casualties.
- More young men die from drink driving incidents than any other group of people.

Source: www.drinkaware.co.uk

Show your understanding

1 What changes have been made to laws regarding alcohol in recent years?
2 Why has new legislation been introduced regarding the consumption of alcohol?
3 Outline three steps the Scottish Government has introduced to tackle the misuse of alcohol.
4 What is the impact of alcohol misuse on the health of the Scottish people?
5 What are the laws on the use of illegal drugs and substances?
6 Describe the laws regarding drink driving.

Develop your skills

7 Study Table 3.2 Road accidents by severity and describe the trends in road accidents of all categories between 1970 and 2011.
8 Study Table 3.3 Reported accidents by type of road and severity (2001–11).
  (a) Compare the trends in fatal accidents on built-up roads with fatal accidents on non-built-up roads.
  (b) Compare the trends in serious accidents on built-up roads with serious accidents on non-built-up roads.
  (c) Compare the trends in slight injury accidents on built-up roads with slight injury accidents on non-built-up roads.
9 Study Table 3.4. Describe the trends in motor vehicle offences recorded by the police between 2002–03 and 2011–12 for the following offences:
  (a) Driving with excess blood alcohol.
  (b) Speeding in restricted areas.
  (c) Seatbelt offences.

Branch out

10 Discuss in groups the extent to which the reduction in road accidents and offences can be attributed to laws on drink driving and road safety.

Chapter 4

The criminal justice system in Scotland

The Scottish court system

How does the court system work in Scotland?

What you will learn:

1 How the court system works in Scotland.

2 Sentencing in Scottish courts.

The Scottish legal system has various different courts which are run by the Scottish Courts Service (SCS). The three main courts in Scotland are:

- The High Court of Justiciary
- The Sheriff Courts
- The Justice of the Peace Courts (formerly District Courts).

High Court of Justiciary

The High Court of Justiciary is Scotland's supreme criminal court with jurisdiction over the whole of Scotland and almost all crimes. This court sits in cities and larger towns throughout Scotland. The High Court has unlimited sentencing powers. Edinburgh and Glasgow have permanent High Court buildings. In other areas the High Court sits in the local Sheriff Court building.

Lord Justice General and the Lord Justice Clerk preside over the High Court. Other full-time judges are known as Lord Commissioners when sitting in the High Court.

The High Court deals with the most serious crimes such as murder, rape, culpable homicide, armed robbery, drug trafficking and serious sexual offences, particularly those involving children. A single judge presides over each case and defendants are tried by a jury of 15 men and women.

Sheriff Courts

There are 49 Sheriff Courts in Scotland, each of which covers a particular Sheriff Court District. These Districts are separated into six Sheriffdoms, which are made up of the various courts in their area. Sheriff Courts deal with most cases that go to court across Scotland. They deal with both civil and criminal law. Sheriff Court can deal with are theft, assault, possession of drugs, soliciting and appeals from the Children's Hearing. Examples of civil cases the Sheriff Court can deal with are separation, divorce or dissolution of a civil partnership, custody or aliment disputes and adoption, among others. In April 2013, the Scottish Government announced that ten Sheriff Courts and seven Justice of the Peace Courts would be closed as part of a cost-saving initiative.

Sentencing in Sheriff Courts

In Sheriff Courts, the sheriff has jurisdiction in both summary and solemn criminal cases. In summary court procedure a sheriff may impose prison sentences of up to 12 months or a fine up to £10,000. Under solemn procedure, that is with a jury, the sheriff may impose an unlimited fine or a maximum custodial sentence of five years. The sheriff also has available a range of non-custodial disposals, principally community service and probation.

Justice of the Peace Courts

Justice of the Peace Courts have replaced District Courts. This is as a result of the Criminal Proceedings etc. (Reform) (Scotland) Act 2007. They are run by the Scottish Courts Service.

A Justice of the Peace Court is a lay court where a Justice of the Peace (JP) who is not legally qualified sits with a legally qualified clerk. The clerk provides advice to the justice on matters of law and procedure. Examples of cases the Justice of the Peace Court can deal with are: some traffic offences, for example driving through a red traffic light, being drunk and disorderly, and assaulting a police officer.

The maximum sentence that a JP may impose is 60 days' imprisonment or a fine not exceeding £2,500. The sentencing powers of the JP Court are the same as those that were in the District Court.

The prosecution of crime

There are two systems of criminal procedure in Scotland: solemn and summary. In solemn procedure, a trial takes place before a judge sitting with a jury of 15 members of the public. All cases in the High Court of Justiciary are tried by solemn procedure. Solemn procedure is also conducted in Sheriff Courts. The alleged offence is set out in a document called an indictment. The judge's role is to make decisions regarding questions of the law and how it applies to the case. The jury's role is to make decisions regarding questions of fact and they may reach a decision by a simple majority vote. In summary procedure in Sheriff Courts, the judge sits without a jury and decides questions of both fact and law. The alleged offence is set out in a document called a summary complaint.

Crown Office

The Crown Office and Procurator Fiscal Service is a civil service department that is responsible for prosecuting crime in Scotland, the investigation of sudden or suspicious deaths and investigating complaints about the police. The Lord Advocate is the head of this department and the chief public prosecutor for Scotland. When a crime occurs, the police write up a report outlining the details of the crime. This report goes to the Procurator Fiscal, who decides whether or not to prosecute. All prosecutions in Scotland are conducted by the Crown Office. Prosecutions in the High Court are conducted by the Lord Advocate, who in 2013 was Rt Hon. Frank Mulholland QC, or the Solicitor General, or by Advocates Depute (also known as Crown Counsel). In all other criminal courts they are conducted by the Procurator Fiscal or one of his deputes, all of whom are legally qualified.

Figure 4.1 Lord Advocate Frank Mulholland

Court of Session

The Court of Session is Scotland's supreme civil court. This court sits in Parliament House in Edinburgh as a court of first instance and a court of appeal. An appeal lies to the UK Supreme Court.

UK Supreme Court

The Scottish Government is unhappy that the UK Supreme Court is undermining the independence and distinctiveness of the Scottish legal system by becoming involved in Scottish criminal appeals. The Supreme Court argues that, as the UK's highest Court of the Land, it can judge Scottish appeals if the accused is appealing under the European Court of Human Rights (ECHR) legislation. In 2010 the Supreme Court ruled that Scotland's Lord Advocate had breached the rights of a Mr Cadder (under article 6, ECHR) in terms of self-incrimination and stated that his conviction was not legal. Again in 2011 Nat Fraser, found guilty of murdering his wife in Elgin in 2003, was allowed to appeal to the Supreme Court even though the Scottish High Court had refused leave for his appeal to go to the Supreme Court. Fraser won his appeal and the Supreme Court ordered that he be re-tried in a Scottish court. This took place in May 2012 at the High Court in Edinburgh, and he was found guilty for a second time.

The Scottish Government has set up an independent review group to examine the role of the Supreme Court and make recommendations for change.

Verdicts in Scottish courts

There are three verdicts that a jury can arrive at in Scottish courts: guilty, not guilty and not proven. Both 'not guilty' and 'not proven' lead to acquittal. English courts do not have the 'not proven' verdict. In June 2012 a consultation was launched on whether Scots law's 'not proven' verdict should be abolished.

The not proven verdict has been criticised greatly over the centuries – the famous nineteenth-century Scottish writer Sir Walter Scott called it 'that b*****d verdict' – as it can potentially allow a guilty person to walk free because conclusive proof that they have committed the crime cannot be established. On the other hand, an innocent person accused of committing a crime could be given the not proven verdict – they too walk free, but they have not been proven innocent, and may have difficulty shaking off the suspicions of others.

Michael McMahon MSP believes that this verdict causes confusion and uncertainty both for victims and accused. He believes that removing the not proven verdict would make it necessary to increase the majority needed to convict. At present eight out of 15 jurors are needed to return a guilty verdict. McMahon argues that 'the principle that all persons are innocent until proven guilty entitles them to straightforward acquittal where the prosecution case against them cannot be proven beyond all reasonable doubt'. He argues that there should be only two verdicts: 'guilty' or 'not guilty'.

The Law Society responded to the consultation. In answer to the question 'Do you support the general case set out above for moving to a two-verdict system? Please give reasons for your choice' the Law Society's response was that 'The Committee questions whether there is any requirement to reform the three verdict system in the absence of detailed research.'

In answer to the question 'If there is to be a two verdict system, should these be (a) "proven" and "not proven", (b) "guilty" and "not guilty", or (c) some alternative system (such as the Yes/No approach outlined)? Please give reasons for your choice' the Law Society responded 'It is noted that in response to Michael McMahon MSP's consultation in 2007 the Committee considered that on the basis that the purpose of a criminal trial is to establish whether the Crown has proved its case beyond reasonable doubt then the most logical verdicts would be "proven" and "not proven".

'The Committee, however, recognises that the verdicts of "guilty" and "not guilty" are well established and widely accepted in other jurisdictions.

'Therefore there is disagreement and debate over the "not proven" verdict.'

Lord Carloway published a report into criminal law and practice on 17 November 2012. In this report the issue of the three verdicts was raised. Justice Secretary Kenny MacAskill said that as a result of this report the need to look at the issue of verdicts had arisen.

Show your understanding

1 From the information above, what are:
  (a) The arguments for abolishing the not proven verdict?
  (b) The arguments for keeping the not proven verdict?

Sentencing in Scottish courts

The most lenient outcomes for someone who has been found guilty would be an absolute discharge or an admonition (a warning). Alternatively, an order to 'find caution' might be imposed. This is when the accused is ordered to pay money as security for their good behaviour over a certain period. This can be for up to one year in the Sheriff Court. At the end of the period, if the accused has been of good behaviour they can apply to the court to have the money repaid.

A range of sentences can be imposed by the judge/sheriff.

Custodial sentences and non-custodial sentences

A custodial sentence is where a person's liberty is restricted. It could be a prison sentence or time in a Young Offender Institution (YOI). A non-custodial sentence is one that does not involve imprisonment.

Imprisonment

The type of court in which the trial was held determines the length of the period of imprisonment that may be imposed. If the accused is aged between 16 and 21, they will be detained in a Young Offender Institution rather than a prison.

Arguments for custodial sentences

- Depriving someone of their freedom is a good form of punishment.
- It acts as a deterrent.
- It keeps people locked up who might otherwise be committing crimes.
- Prisons can help people learn to cope with life outside.

Arguments against custodial sentences

- Prisoners often reoffend on release.
- In March 2012, 2,500 prisoners had served more than ten previous prison sentences, while almost half of those – 1,186 – had served more than 25 jail terms.
- Not enough time or money is spent on rehabilitation of prisoners.
- First-time prisoners could become hardened criminals.

There are two types of prisoner. A sentenced prisoner will have been convicted. A remand prisoner has not been convicted but is being held in prison until charges are heard in court.

Supervised attendance order (SAO)

Instead of serving a period of imprisonment for failing to pay a fine, for example, the court may impose a supervised attendance order. This requires the accused to carry out constructive activities under supervision, such as unpaid work for between 10 and 100 hours, depending on the amount of the unpaid fine.

SAOs have now been replaced by Community Payback Orders (CPOs). This applies to offences committed from 1 February 2011. It also replaces Community Service Orders and Probation Orders. Community-based orders also include the Drug Treatment and Testing Order and Restriction of Liberty Order (electronic tagging).

Case study: Community-based projects

In 2009 a community-based offender project opened in Paisley to tackle persistent offending. The Turnaround Project offers intensive support for young men between the ages of 16 and 30 over an eight-week period.

The project aims to break the cycle of short custodial sentences followed by further offending, typical of many repeat offenders. Such projects intend to reduce the number of short-term prison sentences.

The prison system in Scotland

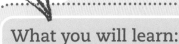

What you will learn:

1 How the prison system works in Scotland.
2 Terms of early release licences.
3 How the chances of reoffending can be avoided.

Scottish prisons

The Scottish Prison Service (SPS) is an agency of the Scottish Government and was established in 1993. There are 14 public prisons and 2 private prisons in Scotland. The total prison population varies from day to day but the average daily number in 2010–11 was 7,852.

It is not only the number of prisoners that changes throughout a year. The SPS employs around 4,000 staff, encompassing a range of careers. The aims of the SPS are to keep in custody those committed by courts, to maintain good order in each prison and to care for prisoners with humanity.

Figure 4.2 Barlinnie Prison

Capacity of Scottish prisons

In April 2010, the design capacity of Scottish prisons was 7,488 with a population of 7,758, whereas on 30 March 2012 the design capacity was 7,848 with 8,295 prisoners. The difference between design capacity and prison population gives an indication of the level of overcrowding.

The Scottish Prison Service Annual Report and Accounts 2010–11 (Scottish Prison Service 2011) notes that: 'Overcrowding limits our ability to deliver the quality of regimes needed to meet prisoner needs and tackle offending behaviour. SPS has no control over the number of offenders sent to prison. Our commitment is to ensure that all those sent are held securely and treated humanely during their time in our custody.'

Early release

Early release is the term given to releasing a prisoner before the end of the sentence imposed by the court.

- Long-term prisoners sentenced to four years or more may be released on licence after serving one-half of their sentence, if this is directed by the Parole Board for Scotland, and must be released on licence after serving two-thirds of their sentence. If the individual is arrested by the police for any criminal action afterwards, the individual can be sent back to jail to complete their sentence.
- Prisoners sentenced to life imprisonment may be released on life licence after serving in full the 'punishment part of their sentence imposed by the court', if this is directed by the Parole Board for Scotland. The Parole Board issues the licence and conditions for the released prisoner.

Facts about some of Scotland's prisons

FACT FILE

HMP (Her Majesty's Prison) Barlinnie

- Receives prisoners from courts in the west of Scotland.
- Retains male prisoners serving sentences of less than four years.
- Manages prisoners serving longer sentences and allocates them to suitable prisons when places become available.

HMP Shotts

- Caters for long-term male prisoners in secure conditions.

HMP/YOI Cornton Vale

- Custodial services for remanded and convicted female offenders including young offenders.
- Provides for all types of sentence and supervision needs.

HMP/YOI Polmont

- Provides custodial facilities for male prisoners between 16 and 21 years of age (in some cases up to the age of 23).
- Prisoners are either convicted or on remand.
- Houses convicted prisoners serving sentences from six months to life.

Reoffending

What works to reduce reoffending?

- ★ The majority of offenders will have desisted from crime by the time they reach their mid twenties or early thirties.
- ★ Offending begins in early adolescence, peaks during the late teens and tapers off in young adulthood.
- ★ Quality social ties formed through employment, marriage or cohabitation and education promote conformity and desistance.
- ★ There are gender differences in the process of desistance from crime.
- ★ Prison can represent value for money in the short term when it is used for high-risk serious and/or certain types of prolific offenders.
- ★ Community sentences are more effective in reducing reoffending than short-term prison sentences.
- ★ According to a systematic review, longer prison sentences are associated with increases in recidivism, which is a term used to describe ex-prisoners who reoffend.
- ★ The effectiveness of swift sentences in reducing reoffending has not been proven.
- ★ Remand can prevent some individuals from reoffending in the short term through incapacitation; however, it is also associated with negative effects that may hinder longer-term desistance.
- ★ Diverting young people away from the criminal justice system can be effective in reducing their reoffending.
- ★ Interventions that aim to increase offenders' sense of agency, self-efficacy and good problem-solving skills are more likely to be effective in reducing reoffending.
- ★ 63% of young people have substance misuse issues on admission to prison.
- ★ Of all prisoners, 80% have the writing skills, 65% have the numeracy skills and 50% have the reading skills of an 11-year-old.
- ★ 25% of these young people have clinically significant communication impairment.

Source: Adapted from *What works to reduce reoffending: A summary of the evidence*, Justice Analytical Services, Scottish Government

Extracts from Tommy Sheridan's prison blog

- I have been moved to a different hall with a semi-open regime. This hall is the first step towards either fully open conditions or the home detention curfew, commonly known as the tag, an ankle bracelet that monitors your movements to ensure you are within your nominated home between the hours of 7pm at night and 7am in the morning.
- With Scottish prisons being so overcrowded and therefore unable to properly implement rehabilitation schemes there is a desire to release low risk offenders into the community and restrict their freedom at home rather than in jail.
- Took part in the hall's 'Man Of Steel' competition yesterday. You run 1,000 metres, take a minute's rest, cycle 3,000 metres, take a minute's rest, then finish with a 1,000 metre row. You aggregate your times over each exercise to arrive at your competition time.
- Among the many improvements to prison life since being moved to the semi-open conditions of Letham Hall is the opportunity to play my beloved Scrabble. Fortunately, a good number of the lads already played the game before I came over from D Hall, so now we have regular games and competitions.
- Back in the Bar-L I will be taking part in a series of comedy workshops over the next five weeks. They are designed to improve prisoner communication skills, confidence, discipline and writing capabilities. At the end of the course we will all be expected to perform in a comedy show in front of the other prisoners.
- It will be a daunting challenge, but surely worthwhile.
- Working alongside excellent comedians like Stu Who? and Stuart Little and being

Figure 4.3 Tommy Sheridan, former Scottish politician

involved in workshops with Frankie Boyle and Kevin Bridges can only be a fun experience. These guys are oozing talent and hopefully the skills learned by fellow prisoners will help in preventing any further offending behaviour.

- The course is effectively a life-skills course that will hopefully equip those who take part with the capacity to avoid future law-breaking. The prison deserves credit for rolling out courses like this alongside the fork-lift driving, joinery, plumbing, anger management, drug and alcohol awareness, anti-sectarian and family bonding courses.
- Prison should not just be about detention. It should also be about rehabilitation. And courses like this can help in that aim.
- If such efforts are not made then prisons will continue to be no more than expensive revolving door institutions with diminishing societal benefits.

Source: http://tommysheridan.wordpress.com/

Show your understanding

1 Describe the changes made by the Scottish Government to the Scottish court system.

2 Describe, in detail, the following adult criminal courts giving examples of sentencing powers and types of crime heard in each court.
  (a) Justice of the Peace Court
  (b) Sheriff Court
  (c) High Court

3 Describe:
  (a) summary procedures
  (b) solemn procedures.

4 **(a)** What are the three verdicts in Scottish courts?
  (b) What changes to the verdict system are advised by Michael McMahon MSP and Lord Carloway? Why do they want change?
  (c) If the 'not proven' verdict is removed, why will there be a need for a greater majority of the jury to return a 'guilty' verdict?
  (d) What opinions does the Law Society hold on these changes?

5 Read the section 'What works to reduce reoffending?'.
  (a) What problems do many offenders face?
  (b) What factors reduce reoffending?

6 Read the extract from Tommy Sheridan's prison blog.
  (a) What efforts are made by the prison authorities to prepare prisoners for release?
  (b) Explain Tommy Sheridan's reference to 'the tag'.

Branch out

7 'This House believes that prison does more harm than good.' Debate.

The Scottish juvenile justice system

Youth justice in Scotland

What you will learn:

1 How the Children's Hearing System works.

2 The work of transitional courts.

The Children's Hearings system is Scotland's unique system of combining justice and welfare for vulnerable and troubled children and young people. The system was one of the radical changes initiated by the Social Work (Scotland) Act 1968, which was incorporated in the Children (Scotland) Act 1995 ('the 1995 Act').

The philosophy of the Children's Hearings system was established in the Kilbrandon Report of 1964. Children and young people who offend and those who require care and protection equally deserve to be considered as children in need and the welfare of the child is paramount.

On 15 April 1971 children's hearings took over from the courts most of the responsibility for dealing with children and young people under 16, and in some cases under 18, who commit offences and/or who are in need of care and protection.

The Children's Hearings system

It is stated on the Scottish Government website that 'Scottish Ministers aim to ensure that every child has the best possible start in life. Those children who commit offences or who have welfare and protection needs require particular help and care.'

The new Children's Hearings (Scotland) Act 2011 ('the 2011 Act') was introduced to Parliament in February 2010 and was enacted on 6 January 2011. The new Act aims to strengthen and modernise the Children's Hearings system and brings into one place most of the children's hearings related legislation. The new system went live on 24 June 2013, replacing the system that was underpinned by the 1995 Act.

The main structural elements of the new Act include the creation of a dedicated body, Children's Hearings Scotland (CHS) whose role is to support the National Convener in the delivery of her functions associated with the recruitment, selection, appointment and training of panel members. The Act also strengthens and promotes children's rights putting the child or young person at the centre of the hearings system.

As set out under section 67 of the Children's Hearings (Scotland) Act 2011, the new 2011 Act, a child or young person may be called to a children's hearing if:

- they are likely to suffer unnecessarily, or the health or development of the child is likely to be seriously impaired, due to lack of parental care
- a schedule 1 offence has been committed in respect of the child
- a permanence order is in force in respect of the child and special measures are needed to support the child
- they have committed an offence
- they have misused alcohol
- they have misused a drug (whether or not a controlled drug)
- they are beyond the control of a relevant person
- they have failed without reasonable excuse to attend regularly at school.

Children under 16 are only considered for prosecution in court for serious offences such as murder, assault which puts a life in danger or certain road traffic offences, which can lead to disqualification from driving. In cases of this kind the Procurator Fiscal has to decide →

if prosecution is in the public interest. Even if so, it is still by no means automatic that the child will be prosecuted. The Procurator Fiscal may refer the child or young person to the Reporter for a decision on whether referral to a hearing is more appropriate.

Where the child or young person is prosecuted in court, the court may, and in some cases must, refer the case to a hearing for advice on the best way of dealing with the child or young person. The court, when it considers that advice, may also refer the case back to a hearing for a decision.

The Children's Reporter

It is stated on the Scottish Children's Reporter Administration (SCRA) website that:

'The SCRA's vision is that vulnerable children and young people in Scotland are safe, protected and offered positive futures. This vision is supported by the Scottish Government and is underpinned by SCRA's values; it ensures that the needs of children and young people are at the centre of everything we do.'

Children and young people are referred to the Reporter from a number of sources, most commonly the police and social work, but other agencies such as Health or Education can make a referral, as well as any member of the public or even the child himself/herself.

When the Reporter gets a referral, s/he must make an initial investigation before deciding what action, if any, is necessary in the child's best interests. The Reporter must consider whether there is enough evidence to support the grounds (or legal reasons) and then decide whether compulsory supervision orders are needed.

The Reporter may:

- decide that no further action is required. The Reporter will write to the child/young person and usually the parent(s) or other relevant person(s) to tell them of this decision.
- refer the child or young person to the local authority so that advice, guidance and assistance can be given on an informal and voluntary basis. This usually involves support from a social worker.
- arrange a Children's Hearing because s/he considers that compulsory measures are necessary for the child or young person. A Children's Panel sits at each hearing.

The Children's Panel

Children's Panels are an important part of the distinctive Children's Hearings system in Scotland. They make important decisions on behalf of vulnerable children who are in need of care and protection. Each panel consists of three lay members of the community who come from a wide range of backgrounds. It must not be wholly male or female and aims to have a balance of age and experience. One of the three panel members will chair the hearing, which is held in an informal setting to make it as comfortable for the child as possible.

Across Scotland there are approximately 2,500 panel members. They are carefully prepared for the task through initial training programmes and they will develop their knowledge and skills during their period of service through experience and attendance at various training events.

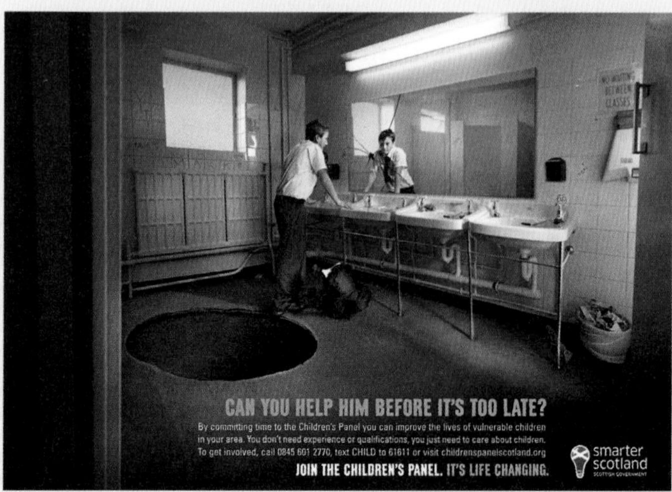

Figure 4.4 A Children's Panel campaign poster

The Children's Hearings process

Supporting the child or young person is at the heart of the hearing process. The hearing considers and makes decisions on the welfare of the child or young person before them, taking account of all the circumstances, including any offending behaviour. The layout of the room is relatively informal and the child or young person can have a person of his or her choosing at the hearing. There will be a report from social workers and possibly from the child's schools, which all are entitled to see.

The hearing can consider cases only where the child/young person and the relevant person(s) accept the grounds or they accept them in part and the hearing decides it is proper to proceed.

Where the grounds are not accepted, or the child does not understand due to age or ability (unless the hearing decides to discharge) the referral, the case is referred to the Sheriff to decide whether the grounds are correct. The reporter will then arrange another hearing.

What decisions may be made?

- The hearing can decide that compulsory measures of supervision are not required and discharge the case.
- The hearing can decide that they need more information to help them make a decision about what is in the best interests of the child or young person and may decide to defer making a decision until a subsequent children's hearing.
- The hearing can decide that compulsory measures of supervision are needed to help the child and can make a compulsory supervision order. The children's hearing may make, vary or continue the order or interim variation order or grant a warrant to secure attendance, only if it considers that it would be better for the child if the order, interim variation or warrant were in force than not.

Compulsory supervision orders

In some cases a child may remain at home but will be placed under the supervision of a social worker. In other cases, the decision will be made to place the child in care, perhaps with other relatives or foster parents, or perhaps in a residential establishment or in secure accommodation if that is necessary.

Source: Adapted from *What is the Children's Hearing System?* Children's Hearings Scotland (www.chscotland.gov.uk/)

Recent research and reports

Recent research evidence has identified issues of concern about some developments within the youth justice system in Scotland.

In their book *The End of an Era? – Youth Justice in Scotland* the authors raise concerns about some developments that have had an impact on the Scottish youth justice system. They discuss issues regarding how these developments undermine the philosophy of the Kilbrandon Report. They state that in recent years there have been many changes to the administration of youth justice which include the restructuring of youth justice interventions, the introduction of antisocial behaviour orders, restriction of liberty orders (RLOs), and electronic monitoring of young offenders.

Another report, 'What Works to Reduce Reoffending: A Summary of the Evidence', makes the following main conclusions:

'Diverting young people away from the criminal justice system can be effective in reducing their reoffending. The deeper a youth is carried into the formal processing system, the less likely he or she is to stop offending.'

Youth/transitional courts

There is a concern about the transition stage when a young person reaches the age of 16 and cases are then heard by the adult courts. A pilot scheme of youth courts has been introduced in Scotland. Two youth courts were established as part of this pilot in Airdrie and Hamilton Sheriff Courts.

Youth courts can be regarded as transitional courts between the Children's Hearing System and the full adult criminal justice system.

Arguments in favour of raising the age of transition

- The transition between Children's Hearings and adult courts is too abrupt.
- Young offenders find it difficult to adjust to adult court.
- The adult courts are not geared to deal with the needs of 16–17-year-olds.
- Many of these young offenders have problems with substance misuse.
- They are often immature and emotionally underdeveloped.
- They have often suffered high levels of victimisation or family relationship difficulties.

Arguments in favour of retaining the age of transition

- 16 is an age when young people generally do reach a sufficient degree of maturity.
- It is both the legal age of marriage in Scotland and also the school leaving age.
- It is argued that the nature and scale of offending among many 16-year-olds makes the adult criminal courts a more appropriate forum than the Children's Hearings System.

Case Study: Time for Change – An Up-2-Us Project

Time for Change (TFC) is a government-funded project aiming to provide an outreach service to high risk, vulnerable girls in the west coast of Scotland. It is a project that prides itself on providing a holistic, relationship-based support service for young women between the ages of 15 and 18 who are at risk of establishing a career that would be dealt with by the criminal justice system. TFC aims to steer the girls from this future, supporting them in many ways to make better life choices using a multi-agency approach which helps young women to receive the most robust and carefully planned care packages. TFC's role within this is to help encourage and sustain the day-to-day practicalities of moving through life, alongside future planning.

It is the flexibility and capacity to meet immediate demands that makes this service vital to the progress of the young women involved, without which many would fall prey to the vicious cycle of the criminal justice system.

A typical day in the life of a project worker

8.30am	*Leave home to attend meeting with social worker regarding new referral. On journey this time is used to: speak to colleagues, confirm those who require to be seen; ensure that there is a relevant focus such as seeking employment or education; time is also used to catch up on any 'on-call' incidents which may have happened during the previous night.*
9.30am	*Meeting with social worker to determine the primary issues affecting the young woman in question, including any future planning. Time for Change role is established and plans are made to meet the girl in question.*

11am	*Visit girl involved in previous night's on-call situation. Attempt to get in contact with said girl fails. Update colleague who is scheduled to visit her later in the day. Phone call to social worker to update her on situation and let her know we will update again once contact is made.*
12pm	*Leave to meet next contact. On journey, receive phone call from residential unit asking if I would have any free time today to visit another young woman whom we have worked with for a substantial period of time. Agree to collect her at 3.30pm and arrange for another TFC worker to cover original contact.*
1pm	*Collect young person from her house. Being only our second contact, use this time to begin 'progress notes' – a form used to identify and monitor potential risks and strengths specific to each individual girl.*
3.30pm	*Travel to meet next contact. Young person had requested to discuss outcome of her Children's Panel review as her Supervision Order had been altered to allow increased home contact. Discussed how she could sustain this contact with the help of TFC. Tried to establish and understand her place within her family. Take her to children's unit to pack some of her belongings and agree to pick her up later to take her to her home.*
5.30pm	*Travel to next contact. During journey use time to speak to colleague who managed to meet the girl involved in a crisis situation the previous night. With the girl safe and the situation under control, will phone social worker the following day to update. Next contact is with a girl who was released from prison one week ago.*
7.45pm	*Once home, use some time to write up 'contact notes' for each contact made that day.*

Show your understanding

1 Describe the Scottish youth justice system, which was set up following the Kilbrandon Report.

2 Describe, in detail, the Children's Hearing System. Include in your answer:
- The Children's Reporter
- The Children's Hearing process
- The Children's Panel
- The decisions that may be made/outcome for the child.

3 'This House would raise the age of transition from Children's Hearings to adult courts to 18 years.' Debate.

4 Read the case study on Time for Change carefully. Write down your thoughts on the benefits of projects like this.

Chapter 5

Poverty and social exclusion

What is poverty?

How can 'poverty' be defined?

It can be very difficult to define the term 'poverty'. On a formal level, a household is considered to be in poverty when the household income is less than 60% of the UK average income.

A further definition of poverty and indicator of inequality is the level of deprivation of material goods. Material deprivation relates to people's ability to buy certain items and participate in leisure or social activities. It relates to households with incomes below 70% of median income and provides a 'material deprivation and low income combined' poverty indicator. This indicator provides a measure of children's living standards which, unlike absolute and relative poverty, is not solely based on income.

What you will learn:

1 How poverty is defined.

2 The difference between absolute poverty and relative poverty.

What is the difference between absolute and relative poverty?

Absolute poverty

We talk about people being in absolute poverty if they do not have the things that are necessary to live, for example food, clothing or shelter. People and even whole households can be in absolute poverty if they live on a low income and cannot afford to buy certain basic goods and services.

Relative poverty

We talk about people and households as being in relative poverty if their income is below an average income compared with other people in the same area. Relative poverty is usually associated with those who are living on a low income and/or relying on benefits. They may be just able to afford to buy the basic things necessary to live but are in poverty relative to someone on a high income. It can mean them not being able to fully participate in social activities and having to go without things that are seen as improving our daily lives, for example a car or family holiday.

The risk of poverty in Scotland is higher than in many other European countries such as the Czech Republic and Slovakia, as shown in Figure 5.1. Currently 170,000 children in Scotland live in poverty.

RELATIVE POVERTY

People are said to be living in relative poverty if their income is so inadequate as to prevent them from having a minimum standard of living considered acceptable. Because of their poverty they may experience multiple disadvantages through unemployment, low pay, poor housing and inadequate health care.

Adapted from the *Joint Report on Social Inclusion 2012*, European Union, 1995–2012

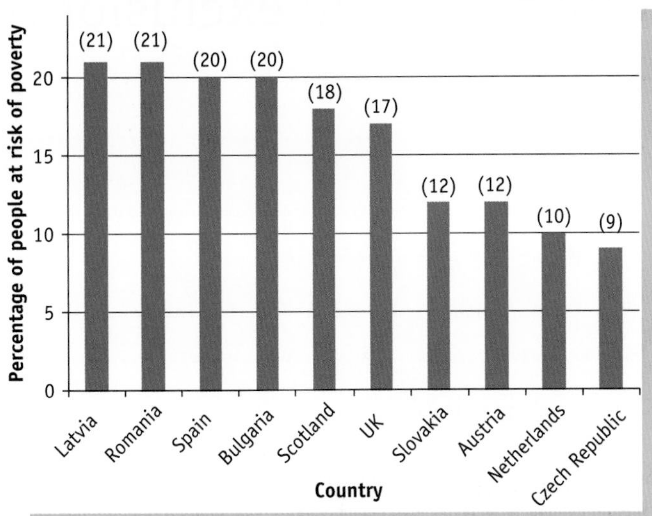

Source: Eurostat, 2011

Figure 5.1 Poverty rates in selected European countries

In the UK, 3.6 million children live in poverty, that's almost a third of children, and one-third are forced to go without at least one of the things they need, such as three meals a day or adequate clothing. In Scotland, 13 councils have wards where around one-third of children live in severe poverty. The worst areas are in Glasgow, North Ayrshire, West Dunbartonshire and Clackmannanshire, as indicated in Table 5.1, which displays the ten Scottish local authority areas with the highest estimates of severe child poverty. This means that in Scotland poverty results in a day-to-day struggle to live and survive for many families.

Local authority area	Percentage of children in severe poverty (estimate)
Glasgow City	18%
North Ayrshire	14%
West Dunbartonshire	14%
Clackmannanshire	14%
Dundee City	12%
North Lanarkshire	12%
Inverclyde	11%
West Lothian	11%
East Ayrshire	11%
City of Edinburgh	11%
Scottish average	**9%**

Source: *Severe Child Poverty in Scotland*, Save the Children, February 2011

Table 5.1 Percentage of children in severe poverty by local authority during 2008–09

Evidence suggests that the main reason for severe poverty is unemployment, with 72% of severely poor children living in households where both parents are unemployed. The consequences are that around one-third cannot afford play equipment such as a bike or football and one in five cannot afford to celebrate their birthday or Christmas.

Case study: Child poverty in West Dunbartonshire

This case study gives a snapshot of child poverty in West Dunbartonshire, with a specific focus on income and education:

- 26% of children in West Dunbartonshire are growing up in poverty, compared with the Scotland-wide figure of 20%.
- Around 2,000 children in West Dunbartonshire live in severe poverty – 14% of all children in the area.

Unemployment and low pay

Unemployment and low wages are at the heart of child poverty in West Dunbartonshire:

- There are 4,900 unemployed people in West Dunbartonshire – 10.8% of the working age population.
- 19.1% of workers in West Dunbartonshire earn less than £7 an hour, just above the national average of 19%.
- 12,300 children in West Dunbartonshire live in households that are dependent on out of work benefits or Child Tax Credit benefits more than the family element.

Educational attainment

Children who grow up in poverty in West Dunbartonshire are far less likely to do well at school than their better off classmates, seriously harming their future life chances and perpetuating the cycle of poverty:

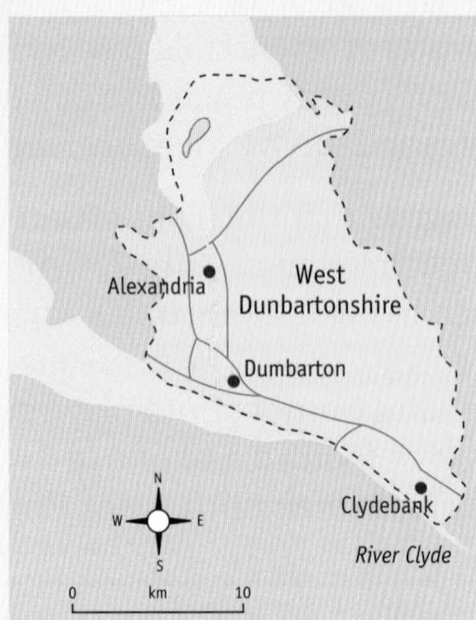

Figure 5.2 West Dunbartonshire

- 28% of primary school pupils in West Dunbartonshire are eligible for free school meals, compared with a national average of 20%.
- At age 16, there is a 16% gap in attainment levels between the poorest pupils and their classmates in West Dunbartonshire.
- 10% of the poorest young people in West Dunbartonshire become unemployed immediately after leaving school.
- 23% of the poorest young people in West Dunbartonshire go to university, compared with an average of 32% across all local authority areas.

Source: West Dunbartonshire Council

Show your understanding

1 What is meant by the term 'poverty'?

2 In your own words describe what is meant by:
  (a) absolute poverty
  (b) relative poverty.

3 Which Scottish local authority areas have the worst levels of children living in severe poverty?

Branch out

4 Look at the Case study: Child poverty in West Dunbartonshire. Using it as a guide, visit the website of your own local authority and complete a similar case study of your own.

Develop your skills

5 'Scotland has one of the highest poverty rates in Europe and this is reflected in the high rates of child poverty in Scottish cities with the City of Edinburgh having the highest child poverty rates.' *(An MEP)* Using Figure 5.1 and Table 5.1, explain to what extent the MEP could be accused of exaggeration.

What is social exclusion?

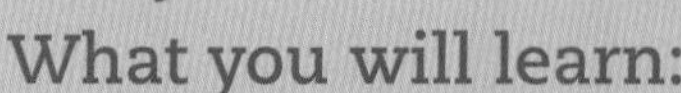

What you will learn:

1 What social exclusion is.

2 Which groups are at risk of social exclusion.

Social exclusion

Social exclusion is a term that allows us to consider poverty in a wider sense than just income. It relates to the extent to which people are prevented from participating in all aspects of society usually because they are living in relative poverty. It also relates to their level of access to services such as education, health and housing.

It is commonly accepted that poverty and social exclusion are the product of low incomes.

Overall, the reality of social exclusion in the UK is that it affects many aspects of people's lives and limits people's access to their fundamental rights. Social exclusion limits the opportunity for people to reach their full potential. For instance, children growing up in poverty are more likely to suffer poor health, do less well at school and become the next generation of adults at risk of unemployment and long-term poverty.

Social exclusion is a lack of basic necessities

I can afford only cheap food; fruit and vegetables to feed children is too expensive; fish is not affordable; healthy food is too expensive for me.

Social exclusion is isolation and depression

I have lost friends as I cannot participate in their activities; even to participate in self-help groups needs money and time; I lack hope and feel powerless.

Source: Voices of people participating in the EU European Meeting of People Experiencing Poverty 2012

What groups may be at risk of social exclusion?

A lone parent family with two children (aged between 5 and 14) is at risk of social exclusion if they are living on less than £256 per week. A couple with two children (aged between 5 and 14) are at risk of social exclusion if they are living on less than £346 a week, which averages out at just over £12 a day for each person.

It is estimated that 61% of children in severe poverty live in a lone parent household, and 39% in a couple household, but the risk of severe poverty is far higher among the former group. Some 60,000 children in lone parent families, 22% of all children living in lone parent families in Scotland, are in severe poverty. This contrasts with 5% of children in couple households.

FACT FILE

Key factors of social exclusion

Some key factors are seen as making a person more at risk of being socially excluded, such as:

- unemployment or having a low-paid job as this limits access to a decent income and cuts people off from social networks
- low levels of education and skills because this limits people's ability to access decent jobs to develop themselves and participate fully in society
- the size and type of family, i.e. large families and lone parent families tend to be at greater risk of poverty because they have higher costs, lower incomes and more difficulty in gaining well-paid employment
- gender – women are generally at higher risk of poverty than men as they are less likely to be in paid employment, tend to have lower pensions, are more involved in unpaid caring responsibilities and, when they are in work, are frequently paid less
- disability or ill-health because this limits ability to access employment and also leads to increased day-to-day costs
- being a member of a minority ethnic group as they suffer particularly from discrimination and racism and thus have less chance to access employment, and have poorer access to essential services.

All these factors create inequality by introducing additional barriers and difficulties, but should be seen within the overall structural context of how the UK chooses to distribute wealth and tackle inequality.

DEMOS: A WIDER LENS

A 2012 report called 'A Wider Lens' by the think-tank DEMOS revealed the full extent of social exclusion and the hardship experienced across Scotland, estimating that 24,000 families experience exclusion, inequality and face severe disadvantage.

It found that Glasgow is the worst-affected area, with more than one in ten families facing severe disadvantage – three times the national average. Families that face four or more major disadvantages – such as low income, unemployment, no educational qualifications, overcrowding, ill health, mental health problems and living in a poor neighborhood – are considered to be 'severely excluded and disadvantaged'.

The report also identified which types of families are more at risk of social exclusion and therefore more likely to experience severe disadvantage. These are lone parents living in large urban areas in social rented housing.

The Chief Executive of Scottish charity Quarriers, said: 'This report paints a truly bleak picture of what life is like for thousands of families across Scotland who experience social exclusion and inequality every day.'

Source: information from *A Wider Lens*, Louise Bazalgette, DEMOS 2012

Figure 5.3 Glasgow City Chambers

ICT task

Go to the DEMOS website www.demos.co.uk/publications/awiderlens. Using the information from the Special Report 'DEMOS: a Wider Lens' above and the website, complete your own mini report on the full extent of social exclusion and hardship experienced across Scotland.

Show your understanding

1 In your own words, describe what is meant by social exclusion.
2 Which types of families are more at risk of social exclusion?

Branch out

3 What groups may be at risk of social exclusion?
4 Describe the key factors that are seen as making a person more at risk of social exclusion.

Chapter 6

Causes and consequences of poverty

What are the causes of poverty?

What you will learn:

1. The causes of poverty.
2. How inequality and discrimination affect people in poverty.

Poverty and inequality

Poverty is caused by many things that are generally linked to inequality. These are a combination of social, political and economic issues and personal choices. While it is difficult to isolate one issue and say that it causes poverty, it is possible to identify certain factors that can make inequality more likely and which can cause some individuals to experience poverty, for example:

- unemployment
- low pay
- the benefits system
- family structure
- gender
- race
- disability.

Unemployment

Unemployment is defined as a situation where someone of working age is not able to get a job but is seeking and would like to be in full-time employment.

Whether a person is unemployed or not makes a big difference to their chances of experiencing poverty. In Scotland, 39% of children in families where no one works are in severe poverty, compared to around 3% of children in families where at least one parent works. Nevertheless, some 25,000 children in households where at least one adult works are also in severe poverty.

As Table 6.1 shows, in Scotland in 2012, 20.6% of households had no one in them who was working. In most cases the out-of-work benefits that these families receive are very low, leaving them well below the poverty line. In fact any household relying on out-of-work benefits struggles to make ends meet, let alone pay for treats or luxuries. Around 72% of children living in severe poverty in Scotland live within these households where the parents do not work and it is this that has been identified as the cause of their severe poverty.

Type of household	% Scotland	% UK
Households with employment	54.2	53.0
Households without employment	20.6	17.9

Source: Office for National Statistics 2012

Table 6.1 Households with and without employment in Scotland and the UK

Figure 6.1 Many families are caught in the poverty trap

Low pay

As stated earlier, people who are employed can experience poverty. This is because some jobs, especially part-time and unskilled jobs, are low paid. As a result those who are low paid can find themselves just above the poverty line even with the addition of family credits and child benefit.

A 2012 Joseph Rowntree Foundation (JRF) report stated that more than 6 million families are caught in poverty because of low pay, and, for the first time since records began, working families in poverty outnumber the 5.1 million jobless households in the UK.

The number of people in part-time work but wishing to work full time has increased from 0.9 million in 2009 to 1.4 million today. Many workers have been forced to go part time in order to retain their jobs and many, especially in the public sector, have had no wage rises since 2010 (in 2013 they received a 1% increase but also a rise in their pension contributions). Around 4.4 million jobs pay less than £7 an hour, which is less than the living wage of £7.45 an hour that is regarded as the minimum needed to provide a basic standard of living (see page 80).

The Conservative/Liberal Democrat Coalition Government made the controversial decision to increase welfare payments to the unemployed by only 1% in 2013 instead of the price index figure which is at least double that figure. This action is part of government reforms of the benefits system.

In 2012, low pay was considered to be £321 per week for a couple with two children. This figure is after deducting housing costs and shows what is left to pay for other needs such as food, heating and social activities.

In 2013, six in every ten working-age adults living in poverty in the UK were from working households. This shows that many employed people need state benefits just to get by. Evidence for this can be found by looking at the number of people who are in work and claiming housing benefit: the number more than doubled between 2008 and 2012 to almost 1 million.

These people living with low pay that is supplemented by benefits also face rising inflation: food prices shot up by almost 33% between 2008 and 2013, while the minimum wage went up by only 12%.

Leading charity Oxfam warned that as a result inequality in the UK is increasing, with low pay, rising unemployment, involuntary part-time working, pay freezes and cuts in benefit levels all leading to the 'biggest real-terms fall in incomes since the mid 1970s'.

Benefits system

Families in severe poverty are more likely to be claiming benefits and tax credits and this is the group that will be most affected by the new welfare reforms (see pages 69–71).

Figure 6.2 shows that, in Scotland in 2012, 280,000 working households were in receipt of tax credits over and above Child Tax Credit. This is more than double the number in 2001 and is equivalent to around 17% of all working-age households.

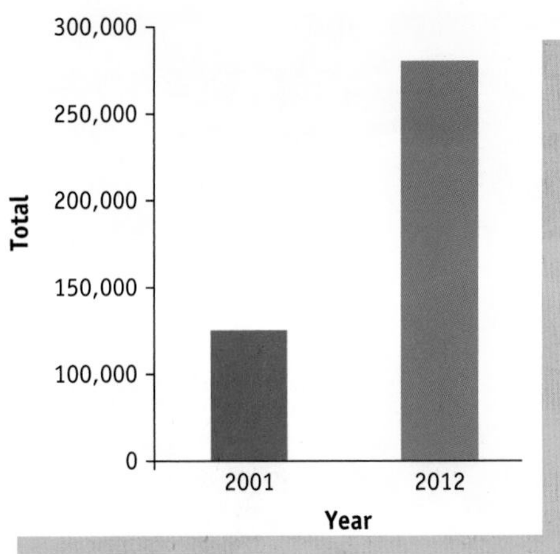

Figure 6.2 Numbers of people receiving Working Tax Credits in Scotland

Figure 6.3 Children living in larger households, with three or more children, are more likely to be living in poverty

Family structure

The size of a family can cause some people to experience poverty. Families with children are more likely to be poor than people without children. This is because costs go up with the birth of a child at the same time as family income goes down with parents cutting back on work or paying for childcare. It is estimated that 30,000 children in severe poverty in Scotland live in households with three or more children, meaning that 12% of children in these larger households are in severe poverty. This compares with 9% of children in smaller households.

The age of the parents in a family can cause some people to experience poverty. For example, children living with parents aged under 25 are more likely to be in severe poverty than those living with older parents. In 2012, 30% of children whose parents were younger than 25 were living in severe poverty.

Show your understanding

1. How would you define unemployment?
2. Give two reasons why employed people can experience poverty.
3. What evidence supports the view that a greater number of employed people are experiencing poverty?
4. What would a couple with two children need to earn to avoid being regarded as low paid?
5. In what way does the size of a family and the age of the parents affect poverty?

Develop your skills

6. Scotland has fewer households in employment compared to the UK but more households with unemployment. *(A politician)*
   Using Table 6.1, explain why the politician can be accused of exaggeration?

Gender

Even though legislation to ensure equal pay has been in place for 40 years (see government policies to reduce gender and ethnic inequalities, pages 59 and 60), the gender pay gap in Britain remains among the highest in the EU. On average, women in the UK earn about 15% less than men. Figure 6.4 shows that women account for two-thirds of all low-paid workers in Scotland.

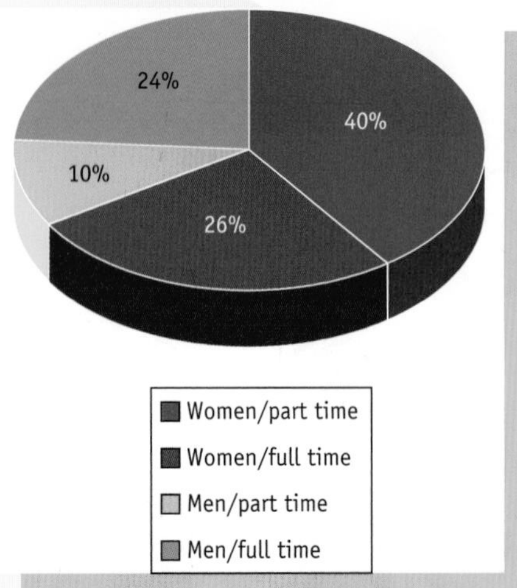

Source: Office for National Statistics 2012

Figure 6.4 Percentage of those paid less than £7 per hour in the UK

Figure 6.5 Many women are employed in low pay occupations, or are less well paid in jobs where men dominate

The pay gap is a clear indicator of gender inequality in the UK today. Progress in closing the gap has been slow and as the age of austerity is taking hold, for the first time the gap is in danger of actually widening.

Many things contribute to gender inequality, including the undervaluing of what is sometimes called 'women's work', where jobs traditionally done by women (such as nursing) are generally less well paid than those where men dominate (such as mechanics).

Also, the lack of flexibility in working hours and opportunities means mothers, who still tend to do most of the unpaid caring for children, can find it hard to mix paid work with family responsibilities.

This 'motherhood penalty' can also lead to outright discrimination, with employers less likely to hire or promote women of childbearing age, for fear they may fall pregnant.

FACT FILE

Women in Parliament

- Currently just over one in five UK Members of Parliament are women, compared with just over one-half of the adult population. The 2010 General Election returned a higher number and proportion of female MPs than any previous general election. Prior to 1987 women had never made up more than 5% of MPs.
- Historically, women found it difficult to be adopted as candidates by the main UK political parties and when they did find a seat, it was likely to be less winnable than those for which men were selected. In the 2005 and 2010 general elections, the all-women shortlist policy appears to have helped change this for Labour and to have broken down the association of candidates' gender and seat marginality.
- The UK has the 15th highest proportion of women MPs out of the 27 EU Member States. In global terms, the UK Parliament ranks 57th out of the 190 countries included in the Inter Parliamentary Union's 31 July 2012 monitoring report. 33% of UK MEPs elected in 2009 are women, compared to 35% of MEPs across all 27 EU Member States.

Source: House of Commons Library

Police force equality fears

Engender, a charity that aims to increase the power and influence of women in society, has voiced concern that only three out of the top 25 posts within Scotland's new single police force have been awarded to females. Of the top five posts only one has been taken up by a woman. Justine Curran, Scotland's only Chief Constable within the current force, failed to achieve any of the top posts.

A spokesman for Police Scotland noted that appointments were made based on candidates' experience and suitability and that 'they were not appointed on the basis of gender.'

Source: information from the *Herald*, 23 January 2013

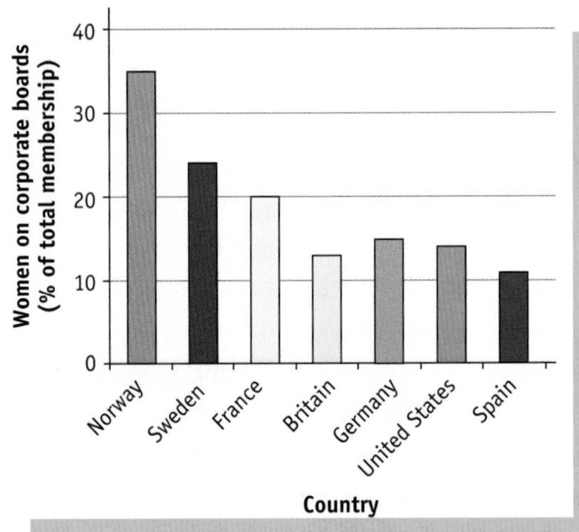

Source: McKinsey Catalyst

Figure 6.6 Women on corporate boards, percentage of total board memberships, September 2011

Government policies to reduce gender and ethnic inequalities

In recent years the UK Government has used a number of strategies to reduce gender and ethnic inequalities. The National Minimum Wage, Working Tax Credit and Child Tax Credit have been used to increase the income of the lowest wage earners. Since many ethnic minority workers and women workers suffer from low-income employment these strategies have been of particular benefit.

Recent governments consider affordable childcare as an important means of reducing the income gap. Child Tax Credit provides a working parent with up to 80% of the cost of childcare up to a maximum of £140 per week for one child and £240 for two or more children.

For women, poverty continues into old age because of interrupted working lives and years spent in part-time employment. Government policies have reduced the number of elderly people living in poverty and the overwhelming majority of these are women. Pension Credit has helped improve the income of women who retire with reduced pension entitlement. Winter Fuel Payment is also paid to most elderly women who have reached the qualifying age.

Equality Act 2010

There are also a number of Acts that try to eliminate sex inequalities and racial inequalities. The Equality Act 2010 replaced nine major equality laws, including the Equal Pay Act 1970 and the Sex Discrimination Act 1975, and around 100 minor laws that existed previously. It covers gender, race, disability, religious belief, age and sexual orientation.

The Equality Act 2010 gives women (and men) a right to equal pay for equal work. The Act requires the Equality and Human Rights

Commission, which was set up under the Equality Act 2006, to work towards the elimination of unlawful discrimination and promote equality.

The Commission can carry out inquiries into the extent and causes of pay differentials in particular areas of employment and can investigate an employer if it thinks that it has pay practices that are discriminatory. The Commission can help individuals to take legal action to enforce their right to equal pay.

The Equality Act also says that companies with 250 or more workers have to publish information about the differences in men's and women's pay. The UK Government plans to do the same for public bodies with 150 or more workers.

The Act also allows for positive discrimination. Job adverts can be aimed at different ethnic groups or women if the organisation does not have enough of that particular group. It can also train these groups to improve their chances of getting a better job with the organisation. The Act allows public organisations such as local councils to use their buying power to influence companies to include equality in the way they work. Public bodies spend £220 billion each year. They can use that power to influence companies that want their business to treat all their employees fairly.

Race

Certain ethnic minorities are also more likely to live in poverty. Race discrimination in the workplace clearly affects income levels.

There seems to be a strong link between ethnicity and low pay or income poverty. In 2012, around 40% of people from ethnic minority communities in the UK were in income poverty. This was twice the rate for white people. More than half of people from Bangladeshi and Pakistani ethnic backgrounds were living in low-income households. In addition, for all ages, people from ethnic minorities were, on average, much more likely to live in low-income households than white people. As Figure 6.7 shows, the income poverty rate varies between ethnic communities.

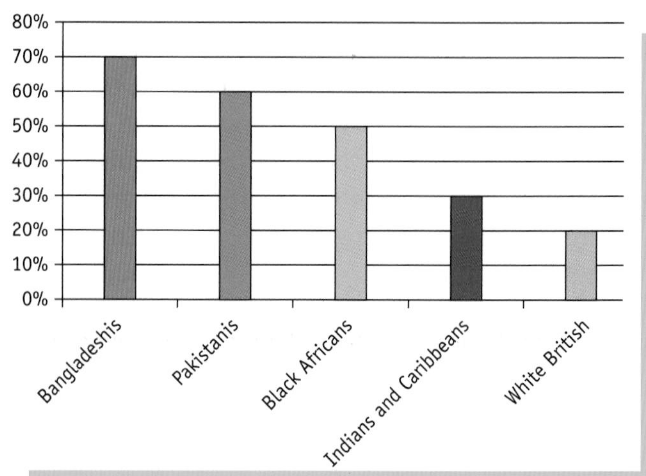

Source: Office for National Statistics 2012

Figure 6.7 Percentage of ethnic community population living in low-income households in the UK

FACT FILE

Inequality by race in the UK

- Black Caribbean pupils are three times more likely to be permanently excluded from school than pupils from any other ethnic group.
- The proportion of white 16-year-olds who do not continue in full-time education is much higher than that for any ethnic minority, but many are undertaking some form of training.
- Black young adults are four times as likely as white young adults to be in prison.
- One in seven adults aged 25 to retirement age from ethnic minorities are not working but want to.
- Around a third of Bangladeshis and Pakistanis are unemployed and say that they do not want paid work, a much higher proportion than for any other ethnic group.
- A quarter of working-age black African, Bangladeshi and black Caribbean households are workless.

Show your understanding

1. Describe in detail the factors that contribute to gender inequality and discrimination around employment and pay.
2. In what ways has the Equality Act 2010 improved equality for women and ethnic minorities?
3. What evidence is there to show that there is a strong link between ethnicity and low pay or income poverty?

Develop your skills

4. 'More women in full-time work are paid less than £7 per hour in Scotland than men. However, the opposite is true for part-time work.' (Benefits Agency spokesperson)

   Using Figure 6.4, give one reason to support and one reason to oppose the view of the Benefits Agency spokesperson.
5. 'While the percentage of ethnic community people living in low-income households is greater than for white British people, it is black Africans who have the highest number living in low-income households.' (Benefits Agency spokesperson)

   Using Figure 6.7, give one reason to support and one reason to oppose the view of the Benefits Agency spokesperson.

What are the consequences of poverty?

What you will learn:

1. How living in poverty affects children and adults.
2. The consequences of poverty for people with disabilities and the homeless.
3. How poverty can affect educational achievement.

Physical consequences

Children who grow up in poverty suffer more persistent, frequent and severe health problems than children who grow up in homes with better financial circumstances.

- Many infants born into poverty have a low birth weight, which is associated with many preventable mental and physical disabilities.
- Children raised in poverty tend to miss school more often because of illness. These children also have a much higher rate of accidents than do other children, and they are twice as likely to have impaired vision and hearing, iron deficiency anaemia, and higher than normal levels of lead in the blood, which can impair brain function.
- Children raised in poverty experience greater personal and family stress.

Addiction

For some people, social exclusion and poverty can increase the risk of acquiring addiction problems. If a person feels socially excluded and trapped in a cycle of poverty and deprivation, feeling unable to change things, they are more likely to turn to alcohol or drugs to feel better.

Disability

Disability is strongly connected to poverty. Parents with disabilities often face multiple barriers to work while children with disabilities place additional demands on the family.

Disability also greatly reduces the in-work rate among female lone parents: 65% among those who are non-disabled compared with just 30% for those who are disabled. Of those who are aged 25 to retirement and are not working, almost half are disabled.

At every level of qualification, the proportion of people aged 25 to 49 with a work-limiting disability who are unemployed is much greater than for those without a disability. Indeed, at 15%, the proportion of people with a work-limiting disability with degrees or equivalent who are unemployed is almost as high as the proportion of people without a work-limiting disability with no qualifications.

% unemployment for or people aged 25–49	With disability	Without disability
Degree	15%	4%
Higher	23%	6%
No qualifications	27%	17%

Source: Office for National Statistics 2012

Table 6.2 Percentage unemployment for people aged 25–49 with or without a disability

Evidence also shows that living in a family with a disabled adult more than doubles the risk of severe poverty for children. In 2012, 19% of children living in a family that had a disabled adult were in severe poverty, compared to 7% in families with no disabled adult. Around a third of children in severe poverty lived with a disabled adult.

According to the Department of Work and Pensions (DWP), most people who have been claiming **key out-of-work benefits** for a long time are sick or disabled. In 2012, sickness or disability was the single most important reason why working-age people claimed out-of-work benefits over a long period. Three-quarters of working-age people receiving an out-of-work benefit for two years or more were classified as sick or disabled.

Key out-of-work benefits: A DWP term which covers the following benefits: Jobseeker's Allowance, Income Support, Incapacity Benefit, Severe Disablement Allowance and Carer's Allowance.

Disability and discrimination

DISABILITY HATE CRIME – IS 'BENEFIT SCROUNGER' ABUSE TO BLAME?

A survey for the disability charity Scope found that almost half of disabled people reported levels of discrimination and public attitudes towards them worsening. They say media coverage about 'benefit scroungers' is turning the public against them. Disabled people reported being 'increasingly confronted by strangers and an increase in resentment and abuse directed at them as they find themselves being labelled scroungers and their right to benefits being questioned'.

Case study: A disabled couple

Kate and William are a disabled couple who live in a small village in the north of Scotland. Owing to their disabilities, both have been unemployed for several years and have mounted up debts. Now, along with most other disabled people, they face a review of their benefits under the new welfare reforms which could cut their income. The couple need to run a car large enough for a wheelchair, as without it they couldn't get out. They can't afford Christmas or birthday presents, and find it hard to heat their home adequately.

We are very worried about the new reviews … if we get less money then we just won't manage. We couldn't. I don't know what we will do.

FACT FILE

The disabled and carers

Employment

- There is a 50% employment rate for disabled people. This falls to 20% for people with mental health problems.
- Longer working lives, and the increasing incidence of disability as we age, means more disability in the workplace.

Women and caring

- There are between 6 and 9 million unpaid carers – a third have never worked, 20% have had to decline work, and many experience poverty in retirement.
- 84% of mothers of disabled children are out of work, blaming the lack of affordable childcare.
- 7,500 children under 16 provide substantial levels of support to their disabled parents.

The Chairman of the Disability Rights Commission (DRC) said, 'The inequality many disabled people experience is felt keenly by others. There is an army of unpaid carers who risk poverty in their retirement. The mothers of disabled children who can't work because there is no affordable childcare. There are thousands of people with mental health problems stranded on benefits with little hope of finding an employer who will take them on.'

Source: Carers UK

Inequality in education

While the Scottish education system serves most children well, some argue that there is a link between growing up in poverty and educational underachievement. Evidence shows that children who grow up in poverty are more likely to do less well at school than their classmates. Children from deprived backgrounds fall behind other children as early as 3 years old – well before school even begins – and many children never catch up.

According to Save the Children, in deprived areas of Scotland 11% of pupils leave school without any qualifications, compared with 3% for the rest of Scotland. On average, there is a 60% gap in attainment levels between children living in low-income households and their better-off classmates at S4. This shows that pupils' social and economic circumstances are the most significant factors explaining their exam results.

The pressures that living in poverty places on families can sometimes mean that parents of deprived children cannot fully get involved in their education, putting them at a further disadvantage to their better-off classmates.

Education is also a key factor in determining the likelihood of experiencing poverty. The lower a person's qualifications, the more likely they are to be unemployed, and if they have a job the more likely they are to be in low-paid work. Therefore, continuing in education after the age of 16, and more so 18, is important in terms of getting a job and avoiding low pay in the future. This explains why the Scottish Government wishes to widen university access for students from deprived backgrounds.

Figure 6.8 shows that the lower a person's qualifications, the more likely they are to be low paid.

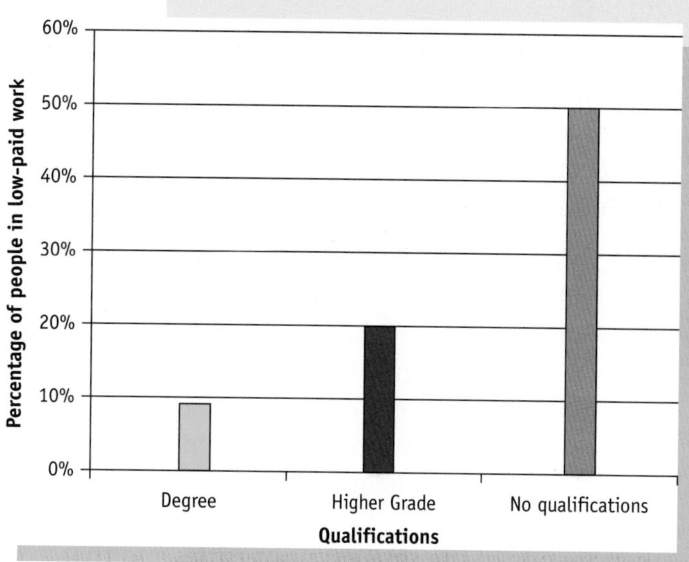

Figure 6.8 Percentage of people in low-paid employment for different levels of qualification

Policies to widen university access

A key educational policy in Scotland is to widen access to Scottish universities for students who live in the most deprived areas of Scotland. This is in response to recent figures which show that Scotland has the worst record for entry to universities among students from poorer backgrounds. Table 6.3 clearly indicates that, despite improvements between 2009 and 2011, there is still a significant gap between Scotland and the rest of the UK.

	2009–10 (%)	2010–11 (%)	% change
UK	30.0	30.6	+0.6
Northern Ireland	39.1	39.4	+0.3
Wales	30.2	31.0	+0.8
England	30.1	30.7	+0.6
Scotland	25.8	27.2	+1.4

Table 6.3 Percentage of entrants to university from deprived areas (socio-economic groups 4–7)

The make-up of Scottish universities

University	%
Total Scotland	27.2
University of the West of Scotland	37.3
Glasgow Caledonian	33.9
Strathclyde	27.2
Glasgow	19.1
St Andrews	15.0

Table 6.4 Percentage of young entrants to university from deprived areas (socio-economic groups 4–7) in 2011–12

Table 6.4 also displays a sharp contrast of intake of entrants from deprived areas between the old universities such as St Andrews and the new universities such as the University of the West of Scotland.

In October 2012 the Scottish Government launched a £10 million initiative to encourage elite universities such as St Andrews to offer in total 700 places to these students. Mike Russell, the Scottish Education Secretary, has criticised these universities for lack of progress. St Andrews has only taken 20 students from this scheme, while Glasgow has taken more than 200. However, St Andrews argue that they are one of the smallest universities and that the problem lies with the poor Higher attainment of these students (see figures from the extract above).

GOVERNMENT ATTACKED OVER TWO-TIER SCHOOLING

An article in the *TESS* by Elizabeth Buie quotes figures from the Scottish Labour leader, Johann Lamont, who states that there is an unacceptable divide between rich and poor in educational attainment:

In 2011 only 220 (2.5%) out of almost 9,000 S5 students who live in the poorest areas achieved three or more Higher passes at A.

Source: information from *Times Educational Supplement Scotland* (*TESS*), 21 December 2012

Figure 6.9 Students graduating from a Scottish university

Show your understanding

1 Describe in detail the physical consequences for children of growing up in poverty.
2 In what ways is disability connected to poverty?
3 Using the Case study: A disabled couple and the Fact File on the disabled, describe in detail the difficulties for disabled people in the UK today.
4 What evidence supports the view that there is a link between growing up in poverty and educational achievement?
5 What action is the Scottish Government taking to improve university entry for students from deprived areas?

Develop your skills

6 'A person with a degree is unlikely to have a low-paid job but there is no difference between those who have no qualifications and Highers.' *(JobCentre Plus spokesperson)*
Using Figure 6.8 explain why the JobCentre Plus spokesperson could be accused of exaggeration.
7 Using Tables 6.3 and 6.4, what conclusions can be made about:
(a) students from the most deprived areas and attendance at UK universities in 2010–11?
(b) students from the most deprived areas and entry to Scottish universities?

Childcare costs

Scottish parents face some of the highest childcare costs in the UK, which are already among the highest in the world. This affects their ability to work, train or study as well as forcing families to make difficult financial choices. Save the Children believes that affordable, accessible and high-quality childcare has a vital role to play in tackling inequality and, more specifically, child poverty. They say that, in order to maximise family incomes, make work pay and, in turn, tackle child poverty and inequality, childcare must become more affordable to parents on the lowest incomes.

A recent survey by Save the Children found that parents living in severe poverty are struggling to access childcare more than other parents, particularly due to the high cost. It also found that parents in severe poverty have cut back on key essentials, such as food and household bills, simply to pay for childcare. A quarter of the parents in severe poverty had given up work, a third had turned down a job, and a quarter had not been able to take up education or training – all because of difficulties in accessing childcare.

I would love to go into full-time work but I just don't see it happening any time soon. I can't afford to … I don't think I'd be able to find a job that would cover my rent and childcare, plus be able to pay the bills and buy the basics. Trying to find suitable childcare is like running into brick walls all the time.

Going without

Families living on a low income generally have to go without certain essential items and are deprived of participating in certain activities.

Figure 6.10 highlights the extent of this problem.

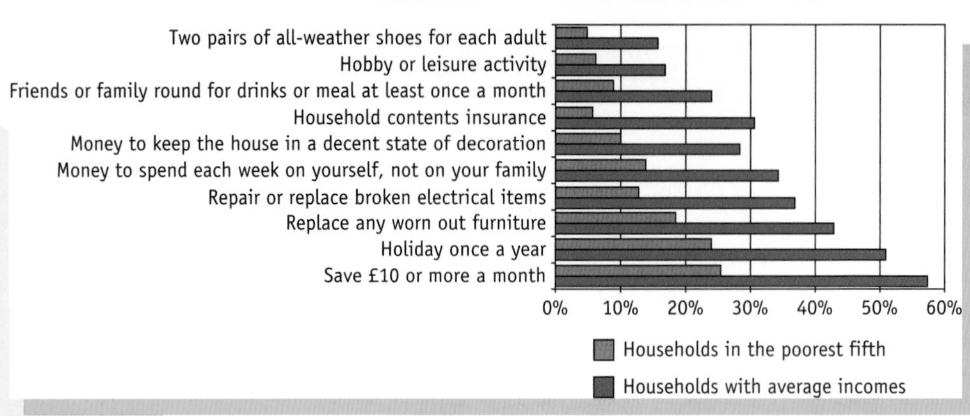

Figure 6.10 Proportion of Scottish families that do without certain items/activities because they cannot afford them

The UK's poorest families frequently face the tightest income squeeze of any group due to the higher rate of inflation and lower wages. Real wages for low-income families in Britain have fallen twice as fast as those of the richest. In real terms, the bottom 10% of wage earners were 3.4% poorer in 2012 than they were a year before compared with a 1.7% drop for the top 10% year-on-year.

According to the Trades Union Congress (TUC), 'People have been getting poorer every month for the last two years as high inflation, tax rises and the dire state of the economy have taken their toll on family budgets. The poorest households have suffered more than anyone else from rising food prices and soaring gas and electricity bills. The Chancellor's obsession with raising VAT, along with swingeing cuts to tax credits, has made life even tougher for those on low to medium incomes'.

Poor housing and fuel poverty

According to the charity Shelter, children living in poor housing – that means temporary accommodation, overcrowded conditions or where the home is damp, cold or infested – suffer from serious and prolonged illnesses brought on by the quality of the houses in which they live. It has found that many of the 1 million children living in poor housing in England are suffering in damp, mouldy and overcrowded homes which are linked to health problems ranging from gastroenteritis and skin disorders to chronic asthma. Doctors reckon that children in poor housing have up to a 25% higher risk of severe ill-health and disability during childhood and early adulthood. Shelter highlights that poor housing increases inequality. Children living in poor housing lose out on vital schooling, endure mental and physical ill-health and fall into a cycle of social exclusion and poverty.

The impact of fuel poverty

A household is said to be fuel poor if it needs to spend more than 10% of its income to pay energy bills. In Scotland, the levels of fuel poverty have been increasing since 2002. In 2012, about one in three households were fuel poor; more than three times the proportion of English households.

Scotland has the second-highest percentage of homes suffering fuel poverty in the UK, 28%, behind only Northern Ireland with 44%. According to the *Herald*, in 2012 Scotland with a population of 5.25 million had 658,000 households in fuel poverty compared with the 331,000 in London, which has a population of 7.5 million.

Fuel poverty leads to inequality and can affect a family's quality of life and health. For example, households on low incomes that have to spend a high proportion of that income on fuel have to go without other things. This can lead to poor diet, or reduced participation in social, leisure and educational activities.

In addition, some disabled people need to have their heating on all the time and rely on electricity to operate stair lifts and other gadgets to help them around the home because of their relative immobility.

Campaign groups have warned that the elderly especially can suffer and have warned that many are being forced to choose between whether they 'Heat or Eat'. Furthermore, the problem has been linked to almost 4,000 deaths a year across the UK.

Kevin, a disabled pensioner and house owner, says:

Because I can't move around I need my heating on all the time to keep warm. Timers are a joke – I need it on all the time.

Homelessness

Homeless children are more likely to be malnourished and miss out on immunisation. Consequently, they generally end up with more health problems.

Homeless women have higher rates of low-birth-weight babies, miscarriages and infant mortality. This could be due to not being able to access adequate prenatal care for their babies as a result of being homeless.

Homeless families experience even greater life stress than other families, including increased disruption in work, school, family relationships and friendships.

Show your understanding

1 Describe the findings of a survey by Save the Children on parents living in severe poverty.
2 In what ways does poor housing affect children?
3 What is meant by fuel poverty?
4 What effect can fuel poverty have on a family's quality of life and health?
5 In what ways does homelessness affect children?

Develop your skills

6 Using Figure 6.10, make and justify three conclusions about the similarities and differences between those on low incomes and those on average incomes who say they cannot afford selected essential items or activities.

Chapter 7

Groups that can help to tackle poverty

Central government

What is the Welfare State?

The Welfare State in the UK is based on the main principle that the government and not the individual has the responsibility to protect the health and well-being of its citizens, especially those in financial or social need, by ensuring that everyone has a minimum standard of living. The modern Welfare State in the UK has its source in the Beveridge Report of 1942 that led to the establishment of a National Health Service and the National Insurance Scheme in 1948.

In 1950, Sam Watson, leader of the Durham coal miners, highlighted the role of the Welfare State when he said, 'Poverty has been abolished. Hunger is unknown. The sick are tended. The old folks are cherished, our children are growing up in a land of opportunity.' Then, as now, its role was to ensure a minimum level of income, health, housing and education below which no one would be allowed to fall: the idea of the Welfare State was a safety net. (See debate over universal and means-tested benefits on pages 72–73.)

What you will learn:

1. How central government helps to tackle poverty and inequality.
2. The various benefits available for different circumstances.
3. Different ways the government can help younger and older people.

Sector	£ billion
EU membership	6.4
Transport	22
Public order and safety	25
Debt interest	44
Defence	40
Education	89
Health	122
Social security	194
Other	140

Source: UK Government

Table 7.1 UK Government spending by sector, 2010–11 (£ billion)

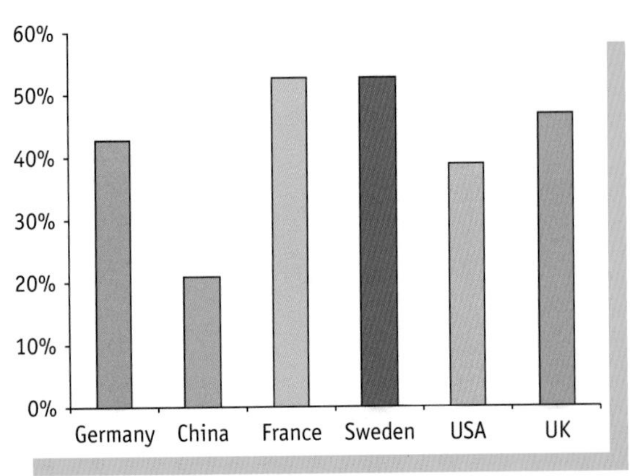

Source: UK Government

Figure 7.1 Government spending as a percentage of gross domestic product (GDP), 2011

The future of the Welfare State

However, the recession of 2008 onwards has led to cuts in public spending, zero growth and rapidly rising unemployment. In 2010 the new Conservative–Liberal Democrat Coalition Government announced that massive spending cuts of £81 billion would need to take place between 2010 and 2015. As Table 7.1 indicates, the annual repayment of debt interest alone is £44 billion. The Scottish Government will witness a reduction of more than £3 billion in its block grant allocation from the UK Treasury in the period 2012–16. Benefits reform and public sector cuts have put pressure on the benefits system, which is already struggling as demand grows. Social services have been reduced while the demand for them is increasing. Social inequalities have widened as the responsibility for welfare is moving away from the state to the individual.

A **Universal Credit** that will combine welfare benefits into one payment will be gradually introduced from 2013 onwards. Its supporters claim it will simplify the system and give individuals greater opportunity to manage their own finances: for example instead of rent payments going direct to the landlord or local authority, the individual will receive this money direct and be expected to manage their budget to ensure payment at the end of the month. However, the fear is that many individuals on low incomes will fail to pay their rent and end up losing their homes.

Money will be paid one month in arrears and the UK Government admits that about 3 million families will see a reduction in their entitlement. Through these measures they hope to reduce the welfare budget by £28 billion.

Universal Credit: A combined welfare credit that will simplify the benefits system by replacing separate payments for Jobseeker's Allowance, Employment Support Allowance, Housing Benefit, Working Tax Credits and Child Tax Credit with one monthly payment.

Welfare cuts

It is expected that between 2013 and 2017 the following are likely:

- Incomes will fall for all those receiving benefits, while the cost of living continues to rise.
- Homelessness will grow as reductions in housing benefit affect more people.
- Personal debt will increase, alongside a rise of payday loan companies. (These companies pay out money immediately to the customer, with no credit check, and can charge interest at over 1,000%!)
- Access to advice and support services, including legal aid and debt advice, will be severely reduced.
- There will be a widening of inequalities between poorer and more affluent areas, as changes to housing benefit push people out of higher-rent areas.
- Many groups, including elderly and disabled people, will suffer from social isolation and insufficient support as services are cut. This will lead to declining physical and mental health, and rising demand for NHS services.
- A growing burden of care will fall on women as access to childcare and social care is reduced.
- Many community and voluntary sector organisations will close down.

Source: British Association for Supported Employment

Figure 7.2 Poorer people can be lured into using pay-day loan shops to borrow money, but at high interest rates

TODAY LABOUR ARE VOTING TO INCREASE BENEFITS BY MORE THAN WORKERS' WAGES

CONSERVATIVES: STANDING UP FOR HARDWORKING PEOPLE

Conservatives

Figure 7.3 A Conservative poster relating to the January 2013 bill

Public opinion

At the same time, public support for the benefits system has been reducing, according to a 2013 report by Ipsos MORI. The report looked at people's views today of Beveridge's five 'giant evils' identified in 1942 – want, idleness, ignorance, squalor and disease. The findings of this report confirm the success of government 'spin' to demonise the unemployed and to divide the nation. In the debates over the Welfare Reform Bill, Conservatives made crude contrast between 'working strivers and feckless skivers' and made reference to those setting out for work looking at 'the closed blinds of their next-door neighbour sleeping off a life on benefits'. Labour voted against the January 2013 bill which restricts benefit increases to 1% a year for three years – a real term cut – and were portrayed by the Conservatives as supporters of the skivers!

Key points: What people think

The proportion of the general public who agree with higher government spending on benefits for those in poverty, even if it means higher taxes, has fallen reflecting a steady decline in support for the benefits system.

- In 2012, 84% of people agreed that stricter tests are needed to ensure people claiming Incapacity Benefit are genuinely unable to work.
- 78% agreed that jobseekers should lose some of their benefits if they turn down work they are capable of doing, even if the job pays the same or less than they get in benefits.
- 62% agreed that people on benefits should have their payments capped if they choose to have 'too many' children.
- 57% agreed that people who receive higher housing benefit because they live in expensive areas should be forced to move into cheaper housing to bring down the benefit bill.

Source: Ipsos MORI

What the parties said in 2012

The Coalition Government

According to the Prime Minister the current benefits system is unaffordable, traps people in poverty and encourages irresponsibility.

He proposed the following reforms, some of which the Liberal Democrats oppose:

- Removing access to housing benefit for anyone between the ages of 16 and 24.
- Banning anyone earning more than £60,000 a year from access to a council house tenancy.
- Breaking the link between benefits and inflation.
- Time-limiting benefits by reducing their levels if someone is out of work for long periods.
- Imposing a new specific cap on housing benefit so that it is worth no more at current prices than £20,000 a year.
- Restricting income support and possibly child benefit to single mothers if they have three or more children.
- Requiring benefit claimants to gain basic literacy and numeracy skills.
- Requiring anyone on employment and support allowance (ESA) to improve their medical condition in return for benefits.
- Requiring lone parents on income support with children as young as three to prepare for work by attending job centres.
- Banning school leavers from going straight onto benefit.
- Paying more welfare benefits in kind, such as free school meals rather than cash.

The Labour Party

The Labour Leader argued that Labour's position on welfare should do more to demand responsibility and reward contribution in the notion of 'contributory welfare'. This is based on two views. The first is the realisation that the Welfare State offers little protection for those who have paid into the system. The second is the hardening of attitudes towards those on benefits, in particular the widespread fear that the system offers a 'free ride' for people who do not work.

FACT FILE

Key welfare reform changes in 2013

- **January** Sliding cuts to child benefit if one parent earns £50,000 or more. Child benefit ends if one parent earns more than £60,000 (see page 74).
- **April** Council Tax Benefit replaced by new system involving 10% cut in funding to councils. SNP Government is shielding Scottish councils from this cut.
- **April** Housing Benefit cut to reflect house size and 'over-occupation': 14% cut for a house with a spare bedroom, 25% cut for two or more extra bedrooms. Around 80,000 claimants in Scotland expected to lose an average of £12 per week. Claimants' options include paying the difference, moving home or taking in a lodger (see bedroom tax pages 74–75).
- **April** Phasing in of replacement of Disability Living Allowance (DLA) with Personal Independent Payments, involving cut of around 20%, which amounts to £260 million in Scotland. An estimated 55,000 people in Scotland are expected to lose DLA.
- **April** Overall benefits cap of £500 per week for couples and £350 per week for single people.
- **October** Phased introduction of the Universal Credit, gradually replacing Housing Benefit, Tax Credits and out-of-work benefits. Will be paid directly to claimants, not landlords, each month, leading to fears of increased homelessness through rent arrears and bad debts.

Source: Audit Scotland Welfare Reforms Update November 2012 and *Sunday Herald*, 6 January 2013

Sample of benefits available to families

- Free school meals are given to children of families receiving certain benefits.
- Childcare Grant is for full-time students in higher education.
- Care to Learn helps pay for childcare while a person is studying.
- Childcare and tax credits are to help pay for childcare costs while a person works.
- Parents' Learning Allowance is for full-time students with children.
- Child Benefit is a payment for each child until they reach 16, or 20 if they stay in education or training.
- Working Tax Credit is a payment to those who work but earn very little.
- Child Tax Credits are for when a person is responsible for one child or more.
- Jobseeker's Allowance (JSA) – including contribution-based JSA, income-based JSA, Income Support.
- Income Support is extra money to help people on a low income or none at all.
- Budgeting Loans are interest-free and can help pay for essential everyday costs.
- Crisis Loans can help with costs after an emergency or disaster.
- Employment and Support Allowance (ESA) money is for when a person can't work because of illness or disability.
- The Christmas Bonus is a one-off tax-free £10 payment to people who get certain benefits.
- Jobcentre Plus provides help when a person leaves benefits and starts work.
- In Work Credit is for lone parents leaving benefits and starting work or self-employment.

Source: www.gov.uk

Benefits – universal or means tested?

At a time when the UK Government is cutting back on public spending to save money and reduce the deficit while more and more people feel the pinch and are worried about money, there are calls for means testing more benefits.

Means testing has been introduced for Child Benefit and is now being suggested for a wider range of benefits, particularly for older people. These include the travel pass and the winter fuel allowance, which are universal benefits to all the elderly.

The Scottish dimension

At present there is a debate in Scotland over the future of universal benefits. Scotland provides some universal benefits that are not available in England, such as free prescriptions and eye tests and no university fees for Scottish students who attend Scottish universities. In October 2012, Johann Lamont, Scottish Labour Leader, spoke about the need to end a 'something for nothing culture'. She argued that with £3.3 billion of cuts to be imposed on the Scottish budgets a review was needed of universal benefits such as free prescriptions and no university fees for Scottish students. However, in a January 2013 speech, Ed Miliband, UK Labour leader, endorsed Labour's support of universal benefits and stated, 'I think that universal benefits that go across the population are an important bedrock of our society.'

SNP Deputy First Minister Nicola Sturgeon said, 'People across Scotland know the importance of universal services such as university education, free prescriptions, free personal care and concessionary travel for older people – and these Scottish Government policies are hugely popular. Johann Lamont wants to axe these benefits through her Cuts Commission, and has also insulted hard-working families and pensioners by branding Scotland a "something for nothing" country.'

Johann Lamont

Nicola Sturgeon

Figure 7.4 Scottish Labour challenges SNP over the affordability of universal benefits

Arguments for more means testing of benefits

- Many people who receive universal benefits don't really need them. Wealthy pensioners do not need a winter fuel allowance.
- It is more important to pay benefits to meet the needs of those living on low incomes.
- It could be considered unfair on those who really need the benefit, if others who don't need it receive it.
- It's unfair that what money there is isn't being properly targeted to those most in need. If that money wasn't being wasted on those who don't really need it, more could go to those who do.
- Harsh cuts are being made to the welfare budget and money should not be given to those who are wealthy; for example should rich pensioners receive a winter fuel allowance or free travel?

Arguments against means testing of benefits

- One of the great strengths of universal benefits is that it is simple and cheap to administer. The opposite is true of means testing. What means testing leads to is a lot more bureaucracy. This can be expensive and inefficient and uses up much of the savings.
- Means-tested benefits aren't actually fair. Many people in need tend to miss out on such benefits. Either they don't know about them, they don't realise they are eligible for them, or they are reluctant to claim them. This is especially true of the elderly.
- When benefits have been universal, people have paid for them in their taxes. A pensioner who wisely has savings should not be penalised for their careful management of income.
- Means testing can be unfair as there is always a cut-off point. Some people who are far from well off and who would 'genuinely' benefit from the payments can be excluded.
- One of the great strengths of universal benefits is that they create a sense of solidarity and ownership in welfare benefits such as Child Benefit or the state pension.

Child Benefit: from universal to means-tested benefit 2013

More than 1 million families considered by the Prime Minister to be better-off lost some or all of their Child Benefit, under rules brought in during 2013. Families with one parent with an income of more than £50,000 lost some of the benefit, and those with one parent earning more than £60,000 had it withdrawn.

By changing Child Benefit from a universal benefit to a means-tested benefit the government is saving money and attempting to reduce the deficit. David Cameron described the move as 'fundamentally fair' but Labour said it was a 'huge assault' on families. Defending the change, the Prime Minister said: 'I'm not saying those people are rich, but I think it is right that they make a contribution. If we don't raise that ... from that group of people – the better off 15% in the country – we would have to find someone else to take it from.'

The Shadow Chancellor said government should tax the richest, rather than make changes that affect those on middle incomes, and described the changes as a 'complete shambles'. A family where the mother stays at home to look after her three children and whose husband earns £60,000 now receives no Child Benefit. Yet her neighbour with one child and both partners working and earning just under £50,000 each, still gets Child Benefit even though their combined income is £100,000!

The bedroom tax

The UK Government hopes to save around £500 million in Housing Benefit by charging council house tenants for their spare rooms. Tenants will have to pay between £11 and £20 a week for bedrooms in their property considered to be in excess of their needs (or downsize to a smaller property). Lord Freud, the welfare minister, considers spare council house bedrooms to be a luxury the country can no longer afford.

People who are judged to be 'under-occupying' their home by one bedroom will have their Housing Benefit cut by 14%. Where they are under-occupying by two or more bedrooms the deduction is 25%. The new criteria for under-occupation could mean that ill or disabled people, who use a spare bedroom for medical equipment, may be affected.

According to the Scottish Government 105,000 households will be affected by the bedroom tax. Of these, 83,000 will be under-occupying by one bedroom and 22,000 will be under-occupying by two or more rooms. With around 586,000 households in the social rented sector, it is estimated that 18% of all households in the sector will be affected. The bedroom tax reduces the amount of Housing Benefit support that can be given to tenants in the social rented sector by introducing new size criteria for working-age Housing Benefit claimants who have extra bedrooms.

Case study: Mrs Brown and her spare room

Mrs Brown is blind and lives in a two-bedroom house. She will get a cut in her housing benefit due to the 'bedroom tax'. She has lived in her home for 20 years and it has been adapted for her needs. Her neighbour acts as a carer for her too. If she is forced to move because she can't afford to stay she will have to leave the community she loves because there are no one-bedroom properties in her area. If she moves away she will leave an area she is able to travel around in safely because she knows it so well.

Mrs Brown's neighbour thinks that the bedroom tax will not be the only hardship. 'With a Universal Credit people will have to budget on a monthly basis instead of weekly. This will cause a further shock to those of us used to juggling our low pay and benefits on a weekly basis. Disability Living Allowance cuts, and Incapacity Benefit reassessment, will further reduce the income of many tenants here. Cuts to Working Tax Credits and council tax benefit cuts will add to everyone's household costs. The overall effect for some families is going to be too much.'

Show your understanding

1 What main principle is the Welfare State based on and what is its role in today's society?

2 What cuts are being made to the UK budget and in what way will they affect Scotland?

3 What is Universal Credit?

4 What are the views of the public and political parties about the welfare reform?

5 Why is the bedroom tax a worry for those who are affected by the changes?

Develop your skills

6 'UK Government spending as a percentage of GDP is far higher than other countries but it is true that our annual debt payment is greater than we spend on defence.' (Jean Devine)
Using Table 7.1 and Figure 7.1, give one reason to support and one reason to oppose the view of Jean Devine.

Debate

7 'Child Benefit should not be a universal benefit and the government action is fair.' Debate. You should use information on page 74 and research using the Internet.

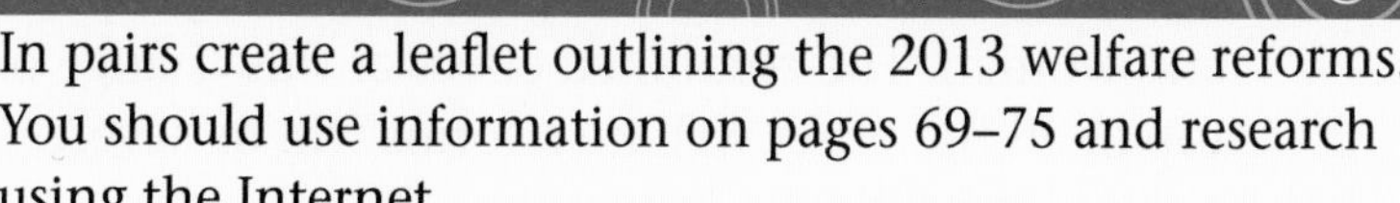

ICT task

In pairs create a leaflet outlining the 2013 welfare reforms. You should use information on pages 69–75 and research using the Internet.

Support for children in families

There are several different benefits for families to help with the extra costs of children. These include benefits for women who are pregnant or who have just had a baby, benefits for the partners of women who have given birth, benefits for people who adopt, and other benefits, tax credits and help to which those who have responsibility for a child or young person may be entitled.

The main benefits for supporting children are Child Benefit and Child Tax Credit. Most people living in the UK can claim Child Benefit for their children.

Many parents can also claim Child Tax Credit for their children. This is payable whether or not the parents are working; it depends on their income and how many children they have.

Child Tax Credit does not include any help with the costs of childcare. However, Working Tax Credit does include some help towards childcare. If a parent is working and is on a low income, they may be entitled to Working Tax Credit.

Parents with a child who is disabled may be able to claim Disability Living Allowance in respect of their child.

If parents are on a low income, they may be able to get other help with the costs of bringing up their children. For example, the children may be entitled to free school meals or help with the costs of school uniform. If the parent is pregnant or has young children, they may be able to get vouchers to help with the cost of milk, fruit or vegetables. In most cases, this help will depend on what other benefits they are receiving.

Source: Citizens Advice Scotland

Child poverty

In an answer to a parliamentary question in January 2013, the Work and Pensions Minister estimated that the reforms 'will result in around an extra 200,000 children being deemed to be in relative income poverty'.

Back in 2006 Mr Cameron said: 'I believe that poverty is an economic waste and a moral disgrace. In the past, we used to think of poverty only in absolute terms – meaning straightforward material deprivation. That's not enough. We need to think of poverty in relative terms, the fact that some people lack those things which others in society take for granted. So I want this message to go out loud and clear: the Conservative Party recognises, will measure and will act on relative poverty.'

Regardless of what Mr Cameron said in the past, the reality according to the Child Poverty Action Group CPAG is that, added to the 800,000 children currently in relative poverty, by 2020 the extra 200,000 children who will sink into relative income poverty due to welfare reforms will mean 1 million children in the UK will be living in relative poverty.

Source: The Institute of Fiscal Studies (IFS) and the *Guardian*

Age of austerity

According to Citizens Advice Scotland capping benefit increases at 1% is an equivalent real-terms cut of 4%. Nearly ten million households – the equivalent of 30% of all households – will be affected. The poorest families will lose the most.

The majority of working-age households in receipt of benefits will be affected by this policy, with an average loss of around £3 a week. This will affect certain groups badly, particularly disabled people and women. The combined effect of this change on top of all the other welfare reforms will be severe. It comes alongside the following:

- reductions in Housing Benefit, particularly for those not using all available rooms (the 'bedroom tax')
- large numbers of disabled people who will have reduced entitlement or no longer be eligible for support through Personal Independence Payment
- the Universal Credit will be less generous to those in work than previously announced
- changes to tax credit eligibility.

Ultimately if welfare changes drive people further into poverty, other problems such as health inequalities, homelessness and family breakdown may occur because of financial pressures. Tackling those problems later could add to the overall public spending bill, not reduce it.

Training, education and Welfare to Work

The Youth Contract

To help tackle youth unemployment the UK Government has a Youth Contract to help young unemployed people get a job. The Youth Contract provides opportunities for 18–24-year-olds, including apprenticeships and voluntary work experience placements. It provides support and help to young people as they move through work experience, the Work Programme and Support for NEETS (Young people not in education, employment or training).

Work experience

The work experience scheme is part of the UK Government's youth contract to help 16–24-year-olds to find work. Under the scheme, which is voluntary, young people are placed with an employer for between two and eight weeks. They receive benefits during this placement, but risk losing their Jobseeker's Allowance for a period of time if they fail to show up after their first week.

Work Programme

The UK Government's scheme to help the long-term unemployed, and those at risk of becoming long-term unemployed, is the Work Programme. It replaced Labour's New Deal and covers all age groups, including young people who have been out of work for more than nine months. Providers appointed by the Department for Work and Pensions (DWP) are given freedom to decide how to support the unemployed, with payments largely based on results. The DWP says: 'They are paid to support claimants into employment and to help them to stay there, with higher payments for supporting the hardest to help.' Providers include private companies and the voluntary and public sectors.

Support for NEETs

Another part of the Youth Contract is support for so-called NEETs – 16–17-year-olds who are not in education, employment or training. Providers have freedom to design a programme that helps these teenagers to move into full-time education, an apprenticeship or a job with training. The providers receive payments by results, depending on how successful they are at helping young people.

The minimum wage

The national minimum wage sets minimum hourly rates that employers must pay their workers. It covers almost all workers in the UK (see Living Wage Campaign on page 80). There are three aged-based rates and an apprentice rate which are usually updated in October each year. See Table 7.2.

Support for older people

Heating allowances

A Fuel Allowance is a means-tested payment under the National Fuel Scheme to help with the cost of heating the home. It is paid to people who are

Year	21 and over	18 to 20	Under 18	Apprentice
2013	£6.31	£5.03	£3.72	£2.68

Source: HMRC

Table 7.2 Minimum wage hourly rates 2013

dependent on long-term benefits and who are unable to provide for their own heating needs. The scheme operates for 26 weeks. Only one Fuel Allowance is paid to a household. The fuel season for 2012–13 started on Monday, 8 October 2012 and finished on Friday, 5 April 2013 (26 weeks).

The Winter Fuel Payment, which is also sometimes called the Winter Fuel Allowance, is an annual tax-free payment of between £100 and £300 which helps people born on or before 5 July 1951 to pay for their heating in the winter. Unlike Fuel Allowance it is a universal benefit. If a person is getting certain benefits, they may be able to also get a Cold Weather Payment. These payments are made when the local temperature is either recorded as, or forecast to be, an average of zero degrees Celsius or below over seven consecutive days. In 2013, the payment was £25 for each seven-day period of very cold weather between 1 November and 31 March.

Big Society

The Big Society was announced by Conservative Party leader David Cameron before the 2010 general election when he became Prime Minister. It then became part of the Conservative–Liberal Democrat Coalition Agreement. It is a general phrase describing the shift of power from central government to communities and to volunteers, and is also said to include charities or non-profit groups taking over the running of some public services. However, the Archbishop of Canterbury dismissed the Big Society initiative as 'aspirational waffle'. He said the idea was 'designed to conceal a deeply damaging withdrawal of the State from its responsibilities to the most vulnerable'.

Show your understanding

1. What benefits for families has the UK Government put in place to help with the extra costs of children?
2. According to Citizens Advice Scotland, what impact will the 2013 welfare reforms have on vulnerable groups?
3. Describe how the UK Government helps with training, education and Welfare to Work.
4. What extra support do elderly people receive?

Scottish Government and local authorities

What you will learn:

1. How the Scottish Government helps with poverty and inequality.
2. How local authorities help young people move from education into work.

Aims of the Scottish Government

The Scottish Government's Child Poverty Strategy for Scotland aims to reduce levels of child poverty, and to ensure that as few children as possible experience any kind of wealth inequality or disadvantage. Central to the strategy is the aim to improve children's wellbeing and life chances – with the ultimate aim being to break inter-generational cycles of poverty, inequality and deprivation.

Employment and training

Ensuring that there are jobs available and that people have the skills to take up these jobs is one way the Scottish Government is tackling child poverty in Scotland.

In 2012 the Scottish Government put in place support for 46,500 training opportunities, of which:

- 25,000 were apprenticeship opportunities
- 14,500 places were to help individuals of all ages who are unemployed to access the labour market
- 7,000 were Flexible Training Opportunities to specifically help meet the needs of smaller employers and businesses.

Opportunities for All

Opportunities for All offers a place in learning or training to all 16–19-year-olds not already in work, education or training. It ensures that all young people have the opportunity to improve their chances of sustainable employment through learning and training.

The Scottish Government helps to improve its skills and training support by introducing incentives aimed directly at supporting Scottish businesses as follows:

The Employer Recruitment Incentive

This initiative offers a £1,000 incentive directly to small- and medium-sized businesses to recruit a participant aged 18+ who has been unemployed for six months or more into a new job. This supports up to 5,000 new jobs for individuals, including those who are participating in Skills Development Scotland's adult pre-employment programme, 'Training for Work'.

Small Business Employment Support Fund

This fund helps companies with fewer than 50 employees to increase recruitment by providing an extra £1,000 subsidy to small businesses which face particular challenges in meeting the miscellaneous cost of recruiting additional staff, such as drafting contracts of employment or setting up or expanding payroll systems.

Help for those on low pay

The main levers for increasing household incomes and reducing pressure on household budgets lie with the UK Government through the tax and benefits system; however, there is a range of measures the Scottish Government has taken in this area. The Scottish Government has funded initiatives to ensure that people receive the benefits to which they are entitled:

- Funding is provided to Macmillan Cancer Support to provide advice to families on how to ensure they claim all the money they are entitled to. This advice is available at the five cancer treatment centres in Scotland and in two NHS Boards for patients with long-term conditions.
- As well as providing financial advice and support, the service also offers targeted provision of employment and vocational rehabilitation support and advice to ensure that, where appropriate, patients are supported to remain economically active during treatment or are assisted to do so after treatment as a part of their overall rehabilitation.
- The Scottish Government's partnership with the Money Advice Service has resulted in a jointly funded programme which helps people deal with problems such as multiple debts, repossession and eviction.

Case study: Healthier, Wealthier Children Project

The Healthier, Wealthier Children Project has been operating in the NHS Greater Glasgow and Clyde area since October 2010 and helps to care for pregnant women and families that are experiencing or are at risk of poverty.

It brings together social care professionals and **third sector providers** of money advice, debt advice, and income maximisation services. Together they offer advice on benefit and tax credit entitlement in relation to fuel poverty, homelessness, addiction, mental health and immigration. Within the health board area ten community health (and care) partnerships and six local authorities are involved in the delivery of the project.

Third sector providers: Providers from the voluntary sector, such as the homeless charity Shelter.

Scottish Social Wage

The Social Wage directly benefits low-paid families. In Scotland it is made up of a range of measures designed to protect people's incomes. Examples include free concessionary travel and prescription charges, no council tax increases, free university education for Scottish students attending Scottish universities and funding for fuel poverty and energy efficiency programmes.

The Scottish Living Wage

The Living Wage is seen by some as helping to reduce inequality and tackle 'in-work' poverty, which afflicts almost one-fifth of all workers in Scotland. Women are particularly vulnerable to low pay and in-work poverty – 43% of workers earning less than £7.00 per hour are women in part-time jobs. In 2012, 17,000 local council workers, the majority of them women, across Scotland were earning a living wage of £7.45 an hour.

Evidence shows that female employment and child poverty are linked. In countries where child poverty is lower than in Scotland there tend to be more women in work. Therefore implementing the Living Wage is an important step in reducing inequality by addressing low pay generally and in particular among women. For instance, in some local authorities where the Living Wage has been introduced more than 80% of the beneficiaries have been female. Paying the Living Wage is seen as a way to reduce inequality and be especially beneficial to low-paid female employees and, in turn, help alleviate child poverty.

Some say that paying the Living Wage is good for business, good for the individual and good for society.

A living wage has been introduced through the Scottish Public Sector Pay Policy. Every employee of the Scottish Government, the NHS and government agencies, receives at least the Living Wage. Employers across Scotland are also encouraged to pay the Living Wage to their employees where they feel they can.

Education

A good education is an extremely important factor in a child going on to succeed in later life. The Scottish Government is tackling child poverty through the implementation of 'Getting it Right for Every Child' and Curriculum for Excellence across Scotland (see also pages 63–64).

Financial education is being offered as part of Curriculum for Excellence, ensuring that all children and young people develop key financial skills. The Scottish Government sees financial education as important to developing the lifelong skills and habits that will enable young people to manage their money effectively in later life, and in time will hopefully lessen the requirement for money advice services and financial advice services being offered to adults in crisis situations.

The Education (Lower Primary Class Sizes) (Scotland) Amendment Regulations 2010 has reduced class sizes to a maximum of 25 pupils in P1 to give all children the best start possible to their education.

The Living Wage Campaign

In 2001, London church groups, charities and trade unionists launched a campaign to persuade employers in both the public and private sector to pay workers a wage well above the minimum wage in order to bring them out of poverty.

Good for business

- Better quality of work from their staff
- Reduction in absenteeism
- Improved recruitment and retention of staff

Good for the individual

- People better able to provide for themselves and their families
- Increase in work quality

Good for society

- Families have been lifted out of working poverty

Help for young people

Community Jobs Scotland

Funding has been provided for Community Jobs Scotland (CJS). CJS helps long-term unemployed young people aged 16–24 into employment. It is

Case study: Community Jobs Scotland – Christy, 21, Impact Arts, Edinburgh

21-year-old Christy joined Impact Arts Edinburgh as a Fab Pad Creative Assistant through the Community Job Fund Programme. Christy had been unemployed for a year after her previous employer was forced to reduce her hours due to the recession. She had applied for 30 jobs and been invited to only four interviews, and was beginning to become disheartened. Christy had always had a keen interest in the arts, taking Art as well as Craft and Design at school and was searching for a position to utilise her skills in these areas. The Community Jobs Scotland positions with Impact Arts were advertised and were ideally suited to Christy's skills and abilities.

In addition to this Christy was also trained in Child Protection and received Challenging Behaviour Support training. One of Christy's favourite aspects of her work involved going on home visits with the interior design team:

'This gives me more of an insight into the Fab Pad Programme and how it works for participants at home. It really helps me to understand the importance of my role in making this happen.'

After three months at Impact Arts Christy had become an integral member of the team. Her confidence working in groups and in one-to-one activities with the participants in the workshops continued to grow daily.

She has enjoyed the challenges of working with young people and feels her age has actually been an asset in understanding the views of the young people she works with:

'I love to support them to work through their challenges. The changes in teenage life even in the short time since I have been a teenager are huge and I want to help people make positive changes.'

Source: Scottish Council for Voluntary Organisations (SCVO)

delivered by the Scottish Council for Voluntary Organisations (SCVO) and Social Enterprise Scotland (SES) in partnership with the Scottish Government. SCVO is responsible for identifying, allocating and monitoring the jobs and SES has responsibility to organise and deliver the additional employability training element.

Modern Apprenticeships

The Scottish Government supports Modern Apprenticeships in Scotland. Modern apprenticeships lead to sustainable employment opportunities, and the apprenticeship programme plays a role in ensuring that young people have the skills required for the Scottish economy now and in the future.

Education Maintenance Allowance

The Education Maintenance Allowance (EMA) benefits around 35,000 young people in Scotland, allowing many from low-paid households to remain in education. The Institute for Fiscal Studies claims that the EMA significantly increases participation rates in post-16 education among young adults, and concluded that its impact is 'substantial'. Nevertheless, in England the government withdrew EMA. Ministers claimed it was scrapped because 90% of previous recipients said that they would have stayed on at school anyway, with or without it.

Improve local communities and areas

Achieving a Sustainable Future: The Regeneration Strategy

This strategy supports disadvantaged communities to promote the wellbeing of residents. Through the People and Communities Fund, money is provided to support community-led regeneration.

Also, the Community Empowerment and Renewal Bill can help communities to own certain public sector assets, have their voices heard in local decisions and tackle vacant and derelict property in their communities.

Source: Scottish Government Annual Report for Child Poverty Strategy for Scotland 2012

Local authorities

Local authorities across Scotland make a valuable contribution to supporting young people as they move from the world of education into the world of work. Local authorities and local employability partnerships work with young people to match training opportunities and other support with local labour market opportunities.

Local authorities and community planning partnerships

Local authorities and community planning partnerships are key partners in supporting young people towards and into work. Local employability partnerships are best placed to understand and respond to challenges specific to their areas. Partnerships work hard to ensure that their provision is aligned to the needs of local labour markets and to reduce duplication between the support they offer young people and that offered by national agencies such as Jobcentre Plus.

Private sector and voluntary organisations

Help from other agencies

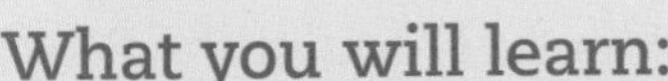

What you will learn:

1. How the private sector can help with poverty and inequality through Modern Apprenticeships.
2. How voluntary organisations can help tackle poverty and inequality.

Private companies can help reduce unemployment and thereby poverty by creating employment opportunities. This is especially true if they get involved with the Modern Apprenticeship scheme.

Also, through Public Private Partnerships (PPP) they can help by working in partnership with the government to improve and regenerate public services. For example, this could be achieved by funding the building of new hospitals and schools.

The voluntary sector plays an important role in supporting the vulnerable in society and publicising their needs to the public and government. Shelter and the Joseph Rowntree Trust are two of the many voluntary organisations with these aims. The number of people turning to different voluntary or charity organisations for help with essentials including food has significantly increased over the last few years. Margaret Lynch, Chief Executive of Citizens Advice Scotland, stated that 'in this recession there has been an exponential increase in the number of working families and people on benefits who are needing help to feed their children and themselves. The national minimum wage has failed to keep pace with the massive increase in food costs over the last five years.'

Across the UK different charities have provided food parcels to those in need. For example, the Trussell Trust charity provided food parcels to around 126,000 people in 2012, more than double the figure in 2010.

JRF monitoring poverty and social exclusion in Scotland 2013

The Joseph Rowntree Foundation (JRF) Report on Poverty and Social Exclusion in Scotland in 2013 highlights real and growing problems – rising poverty among working-age adults without dependent children, rising numbers of people working part-time for want of a full-time job, and high young adult unemployment.

The Citizens Advice Scotland responded:

'This report bears out exactly what [we] see day in and day out. More people unemployed, underemployed or in low-income households who need advice on debt and benefits as they find it increasingly difficult to get through the month and manage to pay the bills and put food on the table. At a time of rising costs it is becoming harder and harder for people to cope and so [we] are increasingly seeing more people in crisis.

'The UK Government's cuts in benefits will take out £2.7 billion from the Scottish economy over the next few years and have a devastating impact on thousands of households across Scotland, those in and out of work, as well as those with disabilities or caring responsibilities. Pushing people further into poverty and financial difficulties will only lead to an increase in other problems such as homelessness, health inequalities, and family breakdown, as well as lead to rising debt and an increase for food hand-outs.' *(Margaret Lynch, Citizens Advice Scotland Chief Executive, 2013)*

One Parent Families Scotland

One Parent Families Scotland is a free, independent helpline for lone parents and anyone affected by the issues surrounding lone parent families. The helpline provides advice on a range of the measures identified in the strategy, such as access to childcare, accessing welfare benefits, and employability advice.

ICT task

'Jobs are this government's top priority and I think youth employment most of all is critical. We have a range of measures to tackle this issue and we are making progress.' *(First Minister)*

By carrying out your own research and using the information in this chapter, copy and complete the table below (the first two rows have been completed for you).

Government initiative	Impact
Opportunities for All	Offers all 16–19-year-olds not in work, education or training a place in learning or training. Ensures that all young people have the opportunity to improve their chances of sustainable employment through learning and training.
The Employer Recruitment Incentive	Offers a £1,000 incentive directly to small- and medium-sized businesses to recruit a participant aged 18+ who has been unemployed for six months or more into a new job. Supports up to 5,000 new jobs for individuals, including those who are participating in Skills Development Scotland's adult pre-employment programme, 'Training for Work'.

Show your understanding

1. What are the two aims of the Scottish Government's Child Poverty Strategy for Scotland?
2. What is the difference between the Scottish Social Wage and the Scottish Living Wage?
3. In what way is paying the Living Wage good for business, the individual and society?
4. Describe in detail how local authorities across Scotland make a valuable contribution to supporting young people as they move from the world of education into the world of work.
5. In what ways can private companies help to reduce unemployment?
6. Describe in detail the ways in which voluntary groups support vulnerable groups of people.

Chapter 8

Health inequalities

Health inequalities

What are health inequalities?

Health inequalities refer to differences in the extent to which groups of people experience health problems, access health services and how long they live. Research has shown that health inequalities are related to factors such as lifestyle choices, social and economic disadvantage, geography, environment, age, gender and race. Those who are most affected are more likely to have poorer physical and mental health than the general population.

Figure 8.1 Factors affecting inequalities in health

What you will learn:

1 What health inequalities are.
2 The many causes of health inequalities.

Who is affected?

People's life expectancy has almost doubled in the UK over the past 150 years, but there are marked variations in the health of different groups. There are gaps between different socio-economic groups, geographic regions and ethnic groups, between men and women, between people of different age groups and between those affected by conditions such as mental health issues. For example, a girl born in London's Kensington and Chelsea area in 2013 might expect to live to about 90, ten years longer than a girl born in Glasgow in the same year.

Current issues

While the overall health of people in the UK is improving, according to the Registrar General, over the last ten years health inequalities between social classes have increased because the health of the wealthy is improving faster than that of poorer people. Poorer people not only die younger, but also have more years of poor health and less access to good health care. There are also inequalities between different age groups and ethnic groups.

Evidence (see Fact file below) suggests that the causes of health inequalities include smoking, diet and exercise as well as poverty, housing, education and access to health care. These include both lifestyle choices, which people have some control over, and other environmental factors over which people have little influence.

Lifestyle choices

Are a person's personal lifestyle choices to blame for health inequalities?

Alcohol

According to NHS Scotland, alcohol sales data suggests that in 2013 consumption had increased by 11% since 1994. In 2012, 23% more alcohol was sold per adult in Scotland than in England and Wales, the widest gap ever.

The impact of this excessive consumption is estimated to cost Scots £3.6 billion each year for health care, which is equivalent to £900 for every adult in Scotland. Hospital admittances due to alcohol consumption have quadrupled since the early 1980s and deaths directly related to alcohol misuse have doubled. The impact on crime and antisocial behaviour is equally bleak, with statistics showing that 50% of prisoners (including 77% of young offenders) were drunk at the time they committed their offence.

FACT FILE

Alcohol consumption facts

- Excessive consumption of alcohol contributes to health problems including high blood pressure, chronic liver disease and cirrhosis, as well as social problems such as antisocial behaviour and violent crime.
- Harmful/hazardous drinking was most common among those living in higher-income households and those living in less deprived areas.
- These associations with income were stronger for women than for men. Women in the highest household income group were twice as likely as those living in the lowest-income households to be harmful/hazardous drinkers (27% compared with 14%).
- Hazardous/harmful drinkers in low-income households consumed more units of alcohol per week than those in higher-income households.
- Similarly, hazardous/harmful drinkers in areas of greater deprivation consumed more units per week than those living elsewhere.
- Around 5% of deaths in Scotland are attributed to alcohol.

Source: NHS National Services Scotland

Smoking

FACT FILE

Smoking facts

- There is a strong link between smoking and a person's social class and levels of deprivation.
- Manual workers are more than twice as likely as those in managerial and professional occupations to smoke (36% compared with 15%).
- For both men and women, smoking rates increase as household income decreases.
- People on lower incomes are almost three times as likely as those on higher incomes to smoke (40% compared with 14%).
- Four in ten adults living in the most deprived areas in Scotland admitted to smoking compared with just one in ten of those living in the least deprived areas.
- The number of cigarettes smoked per day by smokers also increased in line with deprivation, from 12.3 cigarettes in the least deprived areas to 15.2 cigarettes in the most deprived.
- Around a quarter of all deaths in Scotland each year (13,500) are attributable to smoking.
- Smoking is responsible for around 33,500 hospital admissions every year.
- It costs the NHS in Scotland around £400 million to treat smoking-related illness every year.

Source: Scottish Government

Figure 8.2 There is a strong link between smoking and social class

Drugs

FACT FILE

Drugs use facts

- 584 drug-related deaths were registered in Scotland in 2011, which was 1% of all deaths recorded. It is more than in any previous year and an increase of 20% compared with 2010.
- There has been an increase of 76% in drug-related deaths between 2001 and 2011.
- Of the drug-related deaths in 2011, 36% were 35–44-year-olds and 32% were people aged 25–34. Men accounted for 73% of these deaths.
- The NHS Board areas with the largest increases in the numbers of drug-related deaths were Greater Glasgow and Clyde, Lothian and Lanarkshire.
- The percentage increase in the number of drug-related deaths between 2001 and 2011 was greater for women (62%) than for men (57%).

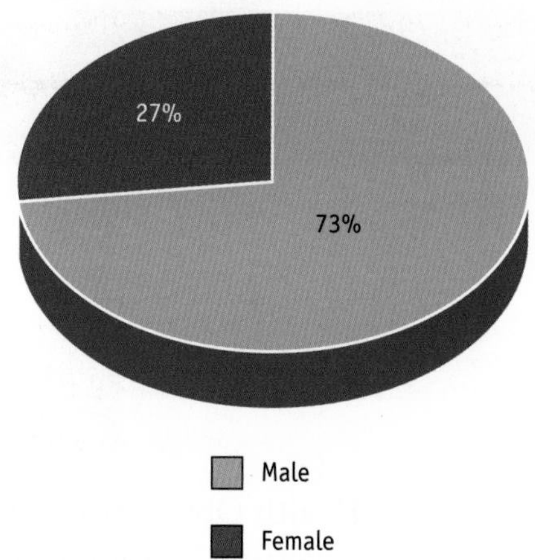

Figure 8.3 Drug-related deaths in Scotland by gender, 2011

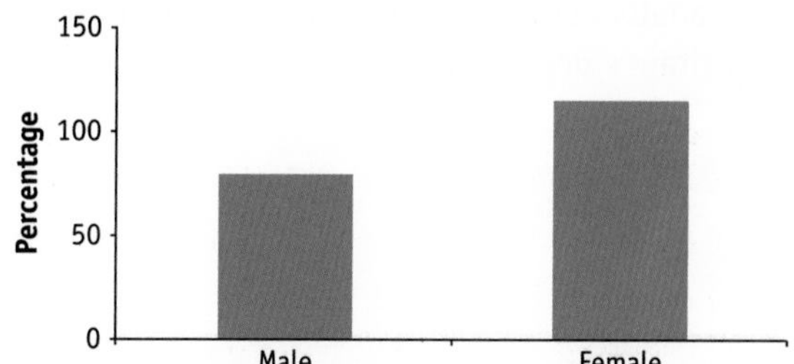

Source: General Register Office for Scotland

Figure 8.4 Increase in drug-related deaths in Scotland by gender, between 2001 and 2011

Obesity

FACT FILE

Obesity facts

- According to the Scottish Health Survey in 2010, 29.9% of Scottish children were overweight or obese; of the 2–15-year-olds, 7.4% were obese and 6.9% were morbidly obese.
- A total of 7,080 men and women were given state handouts last year, claiming they were too fat to work. The Department for Work and Pensions figures also reveal obesity claims have doubled in three years.
- Britain is the fattest country in Europe with one in four adults classed as obese. Hull was recently named as Britain's obesity hotspot.

Figure 8.5 One in four adults in Britain is classed as obese

Social and economic disadvantages: What is the health gap?

The Scottish Government's paper Long Term Monitoring of Health Inequalities 'shows that Scotland's health gap is wider than anywhere else in Europe, and that the poorest Scots are expected to die 20 years before the richest, with men in the most deprived areas having a life expectancy of 68 which is only one year above the retirement age'.

Despite Scotland's overall life expectancy improving, the gap between rich and poor is widening and is wider than in the rest of the UK. In Glasgow, there are huge health inequalities. The Head of the Public Health Observatory said, 'Life expectancy overall is getting better but the inequalities in life expectancy remain very stark.'

People in the most deprived parts of Scotland are four times more likely to die of heart disease before the age of 74 than those in the least deprived, and twice as likely to die of cancer. Among men, the 10% living in the least deprived areas can expect to live until the age of 82, 14 years more than those in the most deprived. Women in the poorest areas live on average to just 67.4 years, compared to 84.6 for those in the wealthiest areas.

On average, girls can expect to live around five years longer than boys in Scotland, although the gap is reducing. Male and female life expectancy is highest in East Dunbartonshire, which includes areas like Bearsden and Milngavie, and lowest in the Glasgow City Council area which includes areas like Calton and Drumchapel. Males in East Dunbartonshire can expect to live for 80 years, eight years longer than in Glasgow City (72 years). Females in East Dunbartonshire can expect to live for 83 years, five years longer than in Glasgow City (78 years).

The gap in healthy life expectancy is even wider. Whereas life expectancy is an estimate of how many years a person might be expected to live, healthy life expectancy is an estimate of how many years they might live in good health. Men in the least deprived areas can expect to reach the age of 70 before experiencing any health problems, compared with just 47 years for those in the most deprived areas. For women, the gap is similar, at 51 years for the poorest and 73 years for the wealthiest.

Scotland's poorest will only be healthy until age 47.

Geography and environment

Does where you live cause health inequalities?

In 2008 a World Health Organization Report on social factors that determine health found that in Glasgow there were serious health inequalities. The report states that a boy in the deprived area of Calton had an average life expectancy of 54 years compared with a boy from affluent Lenzie, 12 kilometres away, who could expect to live to 82.

Two years later in 2010, the journal *Public Health* reported on a study called 'It's not "just deprivation": why do equally deprived cities in the United Kingdom experience different health outcomes?' It went further and said that people from socially deprived areas like Calton had lower life expectancy and poorer health than people from similarly deprived parts of other cities in the UK, for example, Liverpool and Manchester. They called this the 'Scotland Effect' or more specifically the 'Glasgow Effect'.

According to the Glasgow Centre for Population Health, what these reports show is that Glasgow is not alone in experiencing relatively high levels of poor health and deprivation in the UK. Liverpool and Manchester are two other cities which stand out in this regard, with high levels of poverty and the lowest life expectancy of all cities in England. In fact all three cities share similar histories of deindustrialisation, and have high mortality (death rates) associated with deprivation. Experts say that in Scotland the poverty gap has been heavily influenced by the post-industrial legacy in west central Scotland, which is home to many of the UK's most deprived areas.

Therefore, shorter life expectancy in these three cities, and especially in Scotland, is not just due to higher rates of smoking and drinking and a poor diet but is also the result of decades of bad political decisions. The reports claim that it is linked to higher deprivation due to the decline of traditional industries, leading to high unemployment and depression. They attribute Scotland's higher mortality to the political direction taken by the governments of the day, and the consequent hopelessness and community disruption that was experienced as a result.

Other factors, such as alcohol, smoking, drug use, unemployment, housing and inequality are all important, they say, but income inequality, welfare policy and unemployment do not occur by accident, but as a product of the politics pursued by the government of the day.

Case study: NHS Greater Glasgow and Clyde

Health inequalities are noticeable across NHS Greater Glasgow and Clyde where there is a widening gap in health between the richest and poorest people. Women in the least deprived areas can expect to live nine years more than those in the most deprived areas of the city. For men the gap is a staggering 14 years. Social class underlies these differences and when combined with other factors such as gender, race, disability and age, is a major cause of health inequality.

All this means that life expectancy is higher where deprivation is lower. Those in the most deprived areas not only die younger, but spend around ten years more of their lives in poor health compared with those in the least deprived areas of the country.

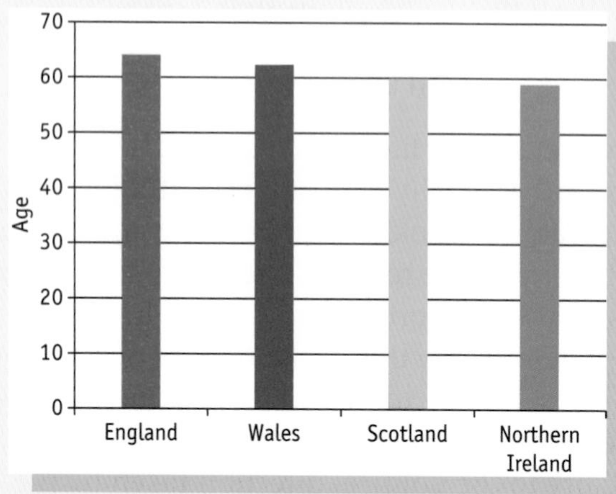

Figure 8.6 Average healthy life expectancy in the UK

General Register Office for Scotland Report

'This report shows that life expectancy continues to vary widely across Scotland. The highest life expectancy is in East Dunbartonshire Council area and lowest in Glasgow City Council area, for both men and women. People living in rural areas, in general, live longer than those in towns. Men in the least deprived areas of Scotland may live 13.2 years longer than those in the most deprived areas while women in the least deprived areas can expect to live 8.9 years longer than those in the most deprived.' *(Registrar General for Scotland)*

What if I reach the age of 65?

I am male and have reached the age of 65. Living in Scotland I can expect to live for a further 17 years. However, because I live in East Dunbartonshire I can expect to live for a further 15 years, eight years more than if I lived in Glasgow City.

I am female and have reached the age of 65. Living in Scotland I can expect to live for a further 19 years. However, because I live in East Dunbartonshire I can expect to live for a further 18 years, five years more than if I lived in Glasgow City.

FACT FILE

Key points

- Health inequalities remain a significant challenge in Scotland.
- The poorest in the country die earlier and have higher rates of disease, including mental illness.
- Tackling health inequalities requires action from national and local government and from other agencies including the NHS, schools, employers and third sector providers (charities).
- Scotland's health is improving. But there are big differences between rich and poor.
- The gap in healthy life expectancy is wide.
- Men in the least deprived areas can expect to reach the age of 70 before experiencing any health problems, compared with just 47 years for those in the most deprived areas. For women, the gap is similar, at 51 years for the poorest and 73 years for the wealthiest.
- More babies born to mothers living in the most deprived areas have a low birth weight than those born to mothers living in the most affluent areas: 9% compared to 5%.
- People struggling with poverty and low income have poorer mental health and wellbeing than those with higher incomes.

National differences

It has been emphasised that there are significant lifestyle differences between Scotland and the rest of the UK. According to Professor Maryon-Davis of the UK Faculty of Public Health, there is 'markedly more smoking, bad diets and drinking in Scotland and Northern Ireland'. Compared with European Union (EU) countries, a Scottish boy can expect to live around four years less than a boy in Sweden and a Scottish girl can expect to live around five years less than a girl in France.

Mental health in later life

According to Age UK, depression is the most common mental health problem among the elderly. In 2013 it was estimated that there were around 2.4 million older people with depression severe enough to impair their quality of life. This number is expected to increase to more than 3 million by 2020.

Dementia

According to the Scottish Public Health Observatory in Scotland (2011) it was estimated that there were approximately 82,000 people in Scotland with dementia. Dementia is more common among older people, but can also affect younger people. According to Alzheimer Scotland, in 2013 around 2,300 people with dementia in Scotland were under the age of 65.

Scottish boys and girls will not live as long as their English neighbours

Scottish boys and girls have the lowest life expectancy within the UK compared to English who have the highest. The average Scottish boy will live to the age of 75.9 while an English boy will live to 78.6. Similarly, Scottish girls will live to the age of 80.4 years, which is 2.2 fewer years than English girls, who are expected to live to 82.6. In Wales and Northern Ireland, the average life expectancy for boys is 77 while girls are expected to live to be 81.

Life expectancy in central Glasgow is the lowest in the UK at just 71.6 for males and 78 for females, whereas in the London area of Kensington and Chelsea it is the highest with males expected to live to 85.1 and females to 89.8.

Source: Office for National Statistics (ONS)

Race

In the UK today black and minority ethnic (BME) groups tend to have poorer health than whites. However, there are also health inequalities between the different groups with some having much worse health than others. Evidence suggests that wealth and income differences among BME groups are the main factor causing race health inequalities.

Ethnic health inequalities

The Health Survey for England (2011) showed that BME groups as a whole are more likely to report ill-health, and that ill-health among BME people starts at a younger age than in the white British population.

- In the UK, Chinese groups have the best health of all ethnic groups including white British people. Pakistani, Bangladeshi and black Caribbean groups have the poorest health, while Indian, Asian and black African people have the same health as white British.
- BME groups tend to have higher rates of cardiovascular disease than white British people, but lower rates of many cancers.
- Race differences in health also vary between generations with levels of ill-health being worse among those born in the UK than in first generation migrants.

Causes of ethnic health inequalities

Many BME groups experience higher rates of poverty than the white British in terms of income, benefits, unemployment, lacking basic necessities and area deprivation and these factors can lead to health inequalities between and within BME groups. However, there are other factors causing health inequalities such as the long-term impact of migration, racism and discrimination, access to health care and differences in culture and lifestyles.

Prevention and dissatisfaction rates

According to Healthcare Commission patient surveys in 2012, the numbers of people from BME groups who stop smoking are generally lower than white groups. On the other hand, the rates of dissatisfaction with NHS services are higher among some BME groups than white groups. For example, Asians report poorer experiences as hospital inpatients.

Examples of ethnic health inequalities

FACT FILE

Cardiovascular disease (CVD)

Men born in Asia are 50% more likely to have a heart attack or angina than men in the general population. Bangladeshis have the highest rates, followed by Pakistanis, then Indians. Men born in the Caribbean are 50% more likely to die of a stroke than the general population, but they have much lower mortality from coronary heart disease.

Source: UK Parliament 2012

Case study: Race and health issues in Scotland

- Mortality varies by race. There is a higher mortality for Scottish-born BME groups compared to those born in England, Wales and Ireland.
- Asian people living in Scotland have been shown to have a higher incidence of coronary heart disease (CHD) but better survival rates than white Scottish people.
- Asylum seekers suffer particularly from mental health problems when they arrive in Scotland. These are compounded by the stress of asylum-seeking status, enforced inactivity and social exclusion. Language is an additional barrier to inclusion.

ICT task

The class should split into groups.

Each group should select a major cause of health inequalities.

Each group should research their cause online and prepare a presentation for the rest of the class.

During each presentation the other groups should take notes on each cause.

Show your understanding

1 In your own words, describe in detail what health inequalities are.
2 Which different groups are most affected by variations in health inequalities?
3 Why have health inequalities increased in the past ten years in the UK?
4 What is the estimated cost to Scots of excessive alcohol consumption each year for health care?
5 Describe the link between smoking and a person's social class and levels of deprivation.
6 Make a list of the main causes of health inequalities.
7 Describe in detail what is meant by the 'health gap'.
8 What is the 'Glasgow Effect'?
9 Describe the differences in life expectancy for males and females who reach the age of 65 in East Dunbartonshire and Glasgow City.
10 What does the General Register Office for Scotland Report show?
11 According to Age UK, what is the most common mental health problem among the elderly?
12 What are the major causes of ethnic health inequalities between BME groups?

Develop your skills

13 'Male drug-related deaths in 2011 in Scotland were higher than female, and also experienced the larger increase.' (Valerie Singleton)
Using Figures 8.3 and 8.4, give one reason to support and one reason to oppose the views of Valerie Singleton.
14 Work in pairs. Using the information in 'Social and economic disadvantages: What is the health gap?' on pages 88–89, each pair should produce a report on the life expectancy of Scots.
15 'It is where you live that causes health inequalities, stupid.' *(John Noakes)*
In groups, research and discuss the view of John Noakes. (You should also refer to the Case study of NHS Greater Glasgow and Clyde on page 90 and the text on pages 89–91.)
16 'While Scottish boys have a lower life expectancy than English boys, Scottish girls live longer than English girls and both boys and girls in Glasgow have a higher life expectancy than those in Kensington and Chelsea.' *(Peter Purves)*
Using only the *Guardian* article, 'Scottish boys and girls will not live as long as their English neighbours' on page 91, explain why Peter Purves could be accused of exaggeration.

Groups that try to tackle health inequalities

What you will learn:

1 How Scottish Government, voluntary sector, local authority and private sector groups try to tackle health inequalities.

The National Health Service in Scotland

Health is a devolved power in Scotland. This means that the Scottish Parliament has primary and secondary legislative powers to run the National Health Service (NHS) in Scotland. However, control over certain areas still remains in Westminster with the Department of Health. These areas include abortion and genetics.

The National Health Service (Scotland) Act 1947 came into effect on 5 July 1948 and created the National Health Service in Scotland to provide free health care as a basic right to anyone living in Scotland.

People living in Scotland have access to a diverse range of health care through the NHS, and both private and complementary medicine practices are available.

The majority of NHS provision is free and any care that is accessed privately is paid for directly or through one of the many private health care insurance schemes available.

NHS Scotland services include:

- hospital treatments
- doctors
- dentists
- opticians.

The NHS in Scotland employs around 158,000 staff including more than 47,500 nurses, midwives and health visitors and more than 3,800 consultants. In addition, there are also more than 12,000 doctors, family practitioners and other health professionals, including dentists, opticians and community pharmacists.

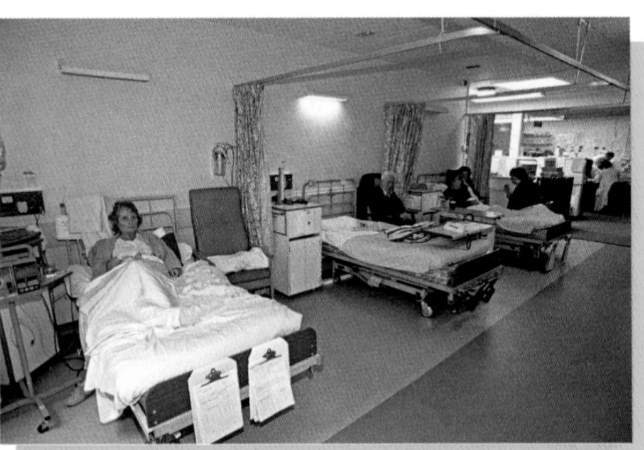

Figure 8.7 The National Health Service (Scotland) provides free health care at the point of need as a basic right to anyone living in Scotland

All NHS Scotland staff work within 14 regional NHS Boards, seven Special NHS Boards and one public health body. Regional NHS Boards are responsible for the protection and improvement of their population's health and for the delivery of frontline health care services. Special NHS Boards support the regional NHS Boards by providing a range of important specialist and national services.

Quality of health care

The Healthcare Quality Strategy for Scotland was launched by the Cabinet Secretary for Health, Wellbeing and Cities in May 2010. This provides the basis for the people who deliver health care services in Scotland to work with partners and the public towards the government's shared vision of world-leading, safe, effective and person-centred health care.

Working in partnership with local authorities and the third sector

NHS Scotland is committed to working closely with partners in local authorities and the third sector through Community Planning Partnerships.

Health promotion and education

Special NHS Boards (NHS Health Scotland – Scotland's health improvement agency)

Special health boards promote ways to improve the health of the population and reduce health inequalities. They offer advice and support to NHS Scotland on delivering equality and diversity, eliminating discrimination and reducing health inequalities. They aim to build a healthier future for everyone living in Scotland by increasing knowledge, providing evidence of effectiveness and developing public awareness of important health messages.

NHS24

NHS24 provides health advice and information over the telephone, 24 hours a day. The NHS24 Health Information Service can give details of all pharmacies, GP practices and dental practices in Scotland to callers. They also have a wide range of information about illnesses and conditions, treatments, NHS services and other support services. They have details about health campaigns and current health issues and can give advice and information on how a person can look after their own and their family's health.

Private health care

There has been an increase in the use of private health care in Scotland. This is partly as a result of more employers offering membership of schemes (such as BUPA or AXA PPP) as part of a package of health care benefits to employees. Nevertheless, the majority of people in Scotland who use private health care do so at secondary care level, that is, they are still registered with an NHS GP. It is when they are referred for specialist treatment or for an operation that they may choose to access private health care.

Figure 8.8 Ross Hall Private Hospital, Glasgow

Examples of private health care use include:

- Patients may be referred straight to a private hospital.
- After a referral to an NHS hospital they might use a private hospital for the actual operation.
- Patients may use a private hospital for only one thing, such as a diagnostic test.

Local authority

Local authorities have a duty to provide community care services within their area. This can include services like residential care homes and care to help an individual remain in their own home.

Community care services

If a person is aged over 65 and looking for help with personal care their local authority will assess whether there is a need for community care services. Personal care is available without charge for residents in Scotland aged 65 and over who have been assessed by the local authority as needing it. However, there may be a charge for any non-personal care such as:

- lunch clubs
- Meals on Wheels
- help with shopping and housework
- non-care related costs of living in a residential care home.

If there is a need for these services the local authority will carry out a financial assessment to determine whether they are able to meet or contribute towards the cost.

Provision and funding

According to research by the National Audit Office (NAO) in 2009, GPs in Wales and Northern Ireland each had 1,538 patients while those in Scotland cared for 1,250 patients each. GPs in England had 1,428 patients each and were paid almost £20,000 more than Scottish GPs.

In the past ten years, spending on health services in the UK has more than doubled from £53 billion in 2000–01 to £120 billion in 2010–11. The NAO said spending had increased consistently across all four countries in the UK, but England spent the least money per person on health services in 2010 to 2011: 'Funding is tighter while the demand for health care continues to grow as a result of an ageing population and advances in drugs and technology.'

According to Scotland's Public Health Minister 'the only way to deal with health inequalities effectively is to address the underlying causes – issues such as negative early years experiences, poverty, unemployment and poor physical and social environments.'

However, Scottish Labour health spokeswoman Jackie Baillie said, 'How long you live should not be determined by the postcode you are born in. It is a scandal that health inequality remains so stubbornly linked to income levels, poverty and deprivation. Poverty traps too many too early and remains too persistent to be tolerated in a country that aspires to be brighter, healthier and fairer. With Scots continuing to have the lowest life expectancy in the whole of the UK, the SNP Government needs to redouble its efforts to tackle poverty.'

Scottish Government policies and initiatives

In Scotland a framework and action plan is being applied which focuses on joint working between the NHS, local government, and the community and private sector. The Scottish Government aims to reduce health inequalities by helping people to sustain and improve their health, especially in disadvantaged communities, and ensure better, local and faster access to health care.

Scotland's health is improving, but there are still many challenges for the Scottish Government to overcome to tackle the country's poor health record. The government has a wide range of initiatives in place to encourage more people to live healthier lives and to reduce smoking, alcohol and drug misuse.

Scotland's Public Health Minister said 'overall, health in Scotland is improving, but health inequalities between our more affluent and more deprived communities still exist. We are taking significant action to cut alcohol consumption, reduce smoking rates, encourage active living, healthy eating, and promote positive mental health. However, the key levers for tackling poverty, such as the welfare system, still lie with the UK Government.'

Reducing smoking rates

The Scottish Government has taken action to stub out smoking, from the 2006 ban on smoking in public places to the ban on displaying tobacco products in shops, to the ban of tobacco sales from vending machines and the raising of the legal age for buying tobacco from 16 to 18.

Changes to the packaging of tobacco products

The Scottish Government has worked with the Department of Health and the devolved administrations in Wales and Northern Ireland to launch a consultation on the standardised packaging of tobacco products. The Tobacco and Primary Medical Services (Scotland) Act 2010 introduced new measures specifically designed to reduce the attractiveness and availability of tobacco to those aged under 18.

In 2012, the Department for Health in England launched a 12-week UK-wide consultation outlining proposals to introduce plain packaging for cigarette

Figure 8.9

products. The consultation document was developed with the support of the Scottish Government and the other devolved administrations in Wales and Northern Ireland. A systematic review of plain packaging conducted in response to the publication of the Department for Health in England's Tobacco Control Plan for England concluded 'that plain packaging would reduce the attractiveness and appeal of tobacco products, it would increase the noticeability and effectiveness of health warnings and messages, and it would reduce the use of design techniques that may mislead consumers about the harmfulness of tobacco products'.

NHS Tayside Quit4U

- Smokers in the poorest areas of Dundee are offered £150 worth of groceries by the health service if they are able to give up cigarettes.
- Participants in the 12-week scheme were given £12.50 a week by NHS Tayside if a carbon monoxide breath test proved they had not been smoking during that time.
- The money was credited onto an electronic card which could not be used for cigarettes or alcohol.

Alcohol Framework for Action

Alcohol abuse in Scotland is on the increase. The Scottish Government is taking action to change cultural attitudes towards alcohol. For example, Alcohol Framework for Action aims to reduce alcohol consumption and harm across the country by enhancing education and diversionary activity, and developing partnership work with the alcohol industry.

Minimum pricing for alcohol

The Alcohol (Minimum Pricing, Scotland) Act was passed in June 2012 and the Scottish Government hopes it will pave the way for the introduction of a preferred minimum price of 50p per unit of alcohol. This policy is supported by many children's charities and is a significant step forward in the Scottish Government's efforts to tackle Scotland's unhealthy relationship with alcohol.

Drugs – the Road to Recovery

The Scottish Government's national drug strategy is called the Road to Recovery. Central to this strategy is the concept of recovery. Recovery is a process through which a person is helped to move on from their problem drug use towards a drug-free life.

Drugs education

Young people need to be able to make informed choices about their lives, and giving them factual, credible and accessible information from reliable sources is vital. Drugs education in Scotland is covered in health and wellbeing education and seeks to build confidence, resilience and good decision-making skills in young people to help them make the right health choices.

The Scottish Government's prevention campaign Know the Score continues to ensure people are aware of and understand the dangers of drugs by presenting them in a factual, non-glamorous and credible way. Know the Score offers information and advice to individuals, parents and carers via a free, confidential 24-hour helpline and website – Choices for Life.

Choices for Life

Choices for Life is a brand new website aimed at all 11–18-year-olds, teachers, youth workers and parents/carers. It is hoped that the website will allow more people to get credible and reliable information on issues such as drugs, alcohol, tobacco and Internet safety.

WWW

To find out more about Choices for Life go to http://choicesforlifeonline.org

The Scottish Government also works closely with the drug experts – the National Forum on Drug-Related Deaths – and other groups from the voluntary sector to tackle the number of drug-related deaths.

Other healthy lifestyle initiatives

A number of other new healthy lifestyle initiatives are reducing health inequalities and supporting the cancer prevention agenda:

- a wide-ranging obesity strategy
- regulations on sunbed use
- the roll out of the HPV immunisation programme
- the development of three social policy frameworks to tackle inequalities in life chances.

The Scottish Government also has policies in place to tackle discrimination, promote the equalities agenda and the reduction of health inequalities. These are:

- NHS Healthcare Quality Strategy
- The Christie Commission
- Equally Well.

The Scottish Government also claims it is taking action across all sectors to tackle social inequality with the launch of two further main initiatives. One of them, called Achieving Our Potential, aims to tackle poverty and income inequality and has been followed up by a Child Poverty Strategy published in March 2011. Another initiative, known as the Early Years Framework, aims to ensure that all children are given the best possible start in life.

NHS Healthcare Quality Strategy for NHS Scotland

Not all people have an equal experience of health services. This highlights the need to take into account individual needs, age, disability, gender and race. The Quality Strategy underpins the Scottish Government's ongoing commitment to equality by ensuring that high-quality health services are provided to everyone in Scotland no matter who they are, or where they live.

Christie Commission

The Christie Commission contributes to NHS Scotland's work to improve the health of individuals and communities, promote equality and reduce health inequalities. For example:

- it prioritises preventative measures to reduce inequalities
- it identifies and targets the underlying causes of inter-generational deprivation and low aspiration.

The commission works with the Equality and Human Rights Commission and the Scottish Human Rights Commission and shares their view that 'no progress towards positive outcomes can or will be achieved without addressing the issue of inequality'. It recognises that there are a disproportionate number of people in Scotland who are vulnerable to discrimination because of their background or status.

Equally Well

Equally Well is the Scottish Government's framework aimed at reducing health inequalities within the Scottish population. It outlines what needs to be done by national and local government, NHS Scotland and the third sector to tackle health inequalities and the underlying reasons for them. The main focus of action is on tackling inequalities that result from socio-economic circumstances. However, it recognises that the causes of health inequalities are complex and that a person's health may also vary because of their age, disability, gender, race or ethnicity, religion or belief and sexual orientation, as well as other life circumstances such as homelessness or history of offending.

In addition, public services reforms have been implemented to enable local agencies and frontline workers to focus on delivering public services, and the public, private and voluntary sectors to work together to improve the quality of life and opportunities for people across Scotland.

Other programmes also offer hope of lasting health benefits, for example the ten-year Go Well programme, which is assessing the health impact of the Glasgow Housing Association's substantial investment in new homes and neighbourhood renewal.

These reforms are based on five strategic objectives: to make Scotland a wealthier and fairer, smarter, healthier, safer and stronger, and greener place.

National parenting strategy

The national parenting strategy encourages agencies to work together to support parents and help them develop their parenting skills.

Figure 8.10 Never too young to learn

The Early Years Framework

The Scottish Government believes that giving children the best start in life will maximise learning for children and young people and will enhance their development with life-long benefits to individual health and wellbeing. The Early Years Framework highlights the importance of all national and local agencies, the third sector and private sector working together to deliver improved outcomes for children.

Case study: Early years/Health inequalities

First Steps Programme, Lanarkshire

The First Steps Programme, which is run by NHS Lanarkshire and South Lanarkshire Community Regeneration Partnership, provides support to vulnerable first-time mothers living in the 15% most deprived areas in South Lanarkshire. The programme addresses health and other inequalities that can impact on a child throughout its life. The aim of the programme is to give the best possible start to the children and so break the cycle of poverty.

Go Play Fund

The Go Play Fund recognises that play is central to how children learn and offers more chances for children aged five to 13 years to participate in free play.

Free prescription charges in Scotland

When the NHS was established by Labour in 1948, all prescriptions were free. Charging was introduced three years later to pay for increased defence spending, and the then Health Secretary Aneurin Bevan resigned in disgust. The SNP administration abolished prescription charges in Scotland in April 2011.

The SNP public health minister said, 'Lifting the charge will save money in the long term, and will no longer put people off going to see their doctor. We believe that free prescriptions are a long-term investment in improving health. If people are put off seeking appropriate care for financial reasons their health will not improve, but if patients can get the treatment they need it will not only help their health but ultimately help to reduce the longer term costs to the health service as well.'

Source: Scottish Parliament

Medical apartheid

However, some see the policy as causing inequality among the home nations of the UK. This is because, while the English are tightening their belts in the wake of the credit crunch, Scotland is spending millions of pounds on free prescriptions. It has been called 'medical apartheid' because the devolved nations enjoy better health services despite paying far less tax per head.

It is claimed that because patients in England still pay for their prescriptions they are subsidising free drugs for those elsewhere in the UK. As well as getting free prescriptions, Scottish people receive free eye tests (compared with an English charge of around £19) and free 'personal care' in old age, while English pensioners have to pay full residential care costs if they own assets of more than £23,000.

The UK Patients Association has long campaigned for free prescriptions in all parts of the UK. A spokesman said, 'We are all paying into the NHS, so why are English patients discriminated against purely on the grounds of geography? It's a postcode lottery of the worst kind, which cuts across the founding principles of the NHS, hitting people who can do nothing about it at their time of greatest need.'

Has the health of Scotland's population improved and have inequalities been abolished?

Health in Scotland is improving and action is being taken to address the health inequalities that exist between rich and poorer communities. These problems are long-standing and will not be solved quickly but effort is being made to reduce alcohol consumption, cut smoking rates, encourage active living and healthy eating, and promote positive mental health.

The Equally Well Report highlighted health inequalities and from that actions were taken to address the underlying causes of poor health that drive inequalities in health. A key theme of Equally Well was the requirement of the Scottish Government to work with and across the public sector and with communities.

EFFECTS OF A FREE PRESCRIPTION COUNTRY

Here is what Professor Keith Oldroyd, director of research and development at the Golden Jubilee National Hospital, Clydebank thinks.

'Under the SNP Government life is a little sweeter. It's a pleasure to drive across the Forth Road Bridge without having to queue at a toll booth. It is the same at the chemist's. I still can't get used to walking out with my prescribed medicines free of any charge. Then there are free eye tests and free bus passes for the over 60s. Good for Scotland. What a place to live. What a place to grow old in, with free personal care for the elderly.

Or is it too good to be true? I'm afraid so. Some Scots are getting less than the best when suffering from life-threatening illnesses. People in the west of Scotland who suffer heart attacks are being deprived of the most effective available drug, ticagrelor. Scotland lags years behind when it comes to introducing new drugs and techniques. And it's down to a shortage of funds.

When treatment is approved, doctors are told to wait because of cost restrictions. By contrast, England and Wales must introduce a new drug within three months after its approval.

Some Scottish health authorities do break ranks. Thus patients in Lothian can get heart treatment denied to those in Glasgow. It's not just a postcode lottery it's a social lottery. The articulate get what they demand while the weak and unknowing get what's going. It's not fair. It's not acceptable and it's not necessary.

The examples are startling. Have a heart attack in Aberdeen and up to 120 minutes later you'll be given a stent – a marvellous device that should extend your life. Anywhere else in Scotland you'll probably be denied a stent after 90 minutes. I know rationing is a reality. But it is shocking when cancer specialists in Scotland cannot prescribe drugs which are seen as standard around the world.'

Adapted from an article by Colette Douglas Home, 'It's not too much to ask: Best care for those in greatest need', the *Herald*, 25 September 2012

What do the Scottish Parties think?

The Scottish Conservative Party Leader said, 'It's well known across the UK that there are free prescriptions in Scotland. What it doesn't tell you is what that costs us. We have seen the number of nurses and midwives reduced by thousands. The people in Scotland are practically paying with their lives for this policy. The free prescription costs take money away from other parts of health spending. One of the contentions we in Scotland have had is that money could be used elsewhere within the health service.'

The Scottish Labour Health spokesperson said, 'I think there is a category of people who earn a great deal of money, who could afford to pay for prescriptions. Universal free prescriptions I think should be reviewed. I think there are better things we could do with the money.'

An SNP MSP said, 'Prescription charges are not a tax on the rich, they are a tax on the sick. Before the SNP abolished them, there were 600,000 people on incomes as low as £16,000 a year forced to pay prescription charges, many of whom we know would avoid collecting prescriptions precisely because of the cost.'

Source: *Scottish Express*, 9 October 2012

Show your understanding

1 What does it mean that health is a devolved power in Scotland?
2 Describe in detail the services provided by NHS Scotland.
3 What does the Scottish Government's Healthcare Quality Strategy for Scotland do?
4 What services does NHS24 provide?
5 How might people use private health care?
6 What are community care services and in what form are they provided by local authorities?
7 How has the Scottish Government taken action to stub out smoking?
8 What is the Tobacco and Primary Medical Services (Scotland) Act 2010?
9 Describe in detail two ways the Scottish Government is taking action to reduce alcohol abuse in Scotland.
10 What does the Scottish Government's drug strategy 'Road to Recovery' aim to achieve?
11 Describe in detail three policies the Scottish Government has in place to tackle discrimination, promote the equalities agenda and reduce health inequalities.
12 Summarise in your own words what each of the three main parties in Scotland say about free prescription charges.

ICT task

1 Using the information in this chapter and your own research, list arguments for and against providing free prescription charges in Scotland.

2 The class should split into groups and each group should carry out research into the following topic: Has the health of Scotland's population improved and have inequalities been abolished?

Each group should report on their findings and conclusions to the rest of the class.

Chapter 9

Assessment: National 4 & 5 Skills and Knowledge

Welcome to National 4 and National 5 Skills and Knowledge!

You should now have the skills and knowledge to complete the assessment demands of the Social Issues in the United Kingdom unit of the Modern Studies course. The skills and knowledge required for National 4 and National 5 are very similar, with National 5 requiring you to handle more detailed sources and to display greater detail in your knowledge answers.

National 4 Assessment

N4

The National 4 award for Modern Studies is assessed by your teacher and not graded by an external examiner. To achieve the award you need to pass the internal assessment for each of the following units:

- Democracy in Scotland and the United Kingdom
- Social Issues in the United Kingdom
- International Issues
- National 4 Added Value: assignment

National 5 Assessment

N5

The National 5 award is made up of internally and externally marked assessments. To achieve the award you need to pass the internal assessment for each of the following units:

- Democracy in Scotland and the United Kingdom
- Social Issues in the United Kingdom
- International Issues

The Added Value for National 5 Modern Studies is an externally assessed course assessment. This consists of two parts:

- National 5 Question Paper
- National 5 Assignment

In Modern Studies we look at a range of issues that affect everyone's lives. These issues are based on evidence gathered by research carried out by a whole series of people and organisations – from the governments to charities. As part of your qualification you will be expected to carry out a piece of personal research on a particular topic which is relevant to what you have studied. This is called the **Added Value unit assignment** at National 4 and the **assignment** at National 5.

How do I carry out a piece of research?

When researching a topic in Modern Studies, it is important to consider where you will get your information from. In the 21st century you have access to huge amounts of information at your fingertips on the Internet. However, you need to be conscious of its accuracy and its likelihood of containing bias.

Where do I gather information from?

The information gathered from research can be broken down into two parts: primary information and secondary information.

Primary information

Primary information is evidence that you have gathered by yourself and is unique to your personal research. Your personal research should be based around at least two pieces of information gathered by primary research as well as information gathered from other sources. The ways in which you gather primary evidence can vary greatly – some examples are below.

- Surveys / questionnaires
- Interviews
- Emails
- Letters
- Focus groups
- Field studies

Secondary information

Secondary information is evidence that you have gathered from research that was carried out by others. You should use it to help support your personal research. There are vast amounts of secondary information available, in many different formats – below are just a few examples.

- Newspapers, magazines and books
- Internet search engines and websites
- Television and radio programmes
- Mobile phone apps
- Social media such as Twitter
- Library books and articles

How do I plan my research?

In order to carry out a successful piece of personal research you need to plan it effectively. You will need to keep all evidence of your planning so that your work can be assessed.

Topic / Issue

You should agree on a topic to research with your teacher. It must relate to one or more of the issues that you have studied in your course, so it is a good idea to pick something from one of the three units you have studied:

- Democracy in Scotland and the United Kingdom
- Social Issues in the United Kingdom
- International Issues

Hypothesis

If you are being presented at National 5 and you have decided on your topic/issue, then you will have to state a hypothesis which you will revisit in your conclusion. A hypothesis is simply a statement that your personal research will try to prove or disprove.

Sources of information

You may wish to consider the following questions about your primary and secondary sources.

- What useful information have I got from this source to help me research my issue?
- How did I collect this information or where did it come from?
- How reliable is the information gathered from the source?
- Could the source contain bias or exaggeration?

Background knowledge

What relevant knowledge do you have from your Modern Studies course which will help you research your issue?

Conclusions

Using all of the information gathered, what are your final thoughts on your issue?

Presentation

How are you going to present your sources and findings?

You could choose the following methods of presenting your Added Value assignment:

- **Oral presentation** – you may want to give a 5-minute talk to the class. This talk should be well organised and can be supported with other materials such as a PowerPoint or Prezi. You could include a question and answer session at the end of your presentation.

- **Written report** – you may wish to submit a structured essay/report or mock newspaper article. You could also create an online blog or wiki to present your findings.
- **Display** – you could create a large and well-structured poster incorporating your findings. After presenting it to the class you could hold a question and answer session.
- **Audio recording** – you could create a scripted podcast to present your findings. The podcast could include interviews or could take the form of a radio broadcast.
- **Video recording** – you may want to create a video recording to help present your findings. You could create a mock news broadcast or a short film and even use software such as iMovie and Movie Maker to aid your presentation.

Sample plan

Below is an example of how a piece of personal research could be planned and structured. You should work with your teacher to consider how you should structure, plan and carry out your own piece of research.

Poster presentation

Area of course: Social Issues in the United Kingdom

Topic / Issue: The effects of poverty on health

Hypothesis: *Poverty is the major cause of health inequalities in Scotland*

Introduction: In this section I will explain why I chose the topic and how I collected my information.

Display: In my poster I will include 4 sources of information – the results of a survey/ questionnaire, the transcript of an interview with a focus group, a section on secondary sources I used and, lastly, a section on my own knowledge.

Source 1 – Survey / Questionnaire

I am going to ask my friends, neighbours and family to respond to the following questionnaire. From the questionnaire I will create a bar graph of responses to the key question. I will then give some of the reasons for people's responses and discuss whether the findings of the questionnaire agree or disagree with my hypothesis. Using the questionnaire, I could also gather evidence to show whether people believe poverty is the major cause of health inequalities in Scotland.

This is what my survey may look like:

<table>
<tr><td>Gender</td><td></td><td colspan="2">Male</td><td colspan="2">Female</td></tr>
<tr><td>Age</td><td>12-17</td><td>18-24</td><td>25-40</td><td>41-60</td><td>60+</td></tr>
<tr><td colspan="3">Do you think that poverty is a major cause of health inequalities?</td><td>Yes</td><td>No</td><td>Undecided</td></tr>
<tr><td colspan="3">Give one reason for your answer</td><td colspan="3"></td></tr>
</table>

This is what my graph may look like:

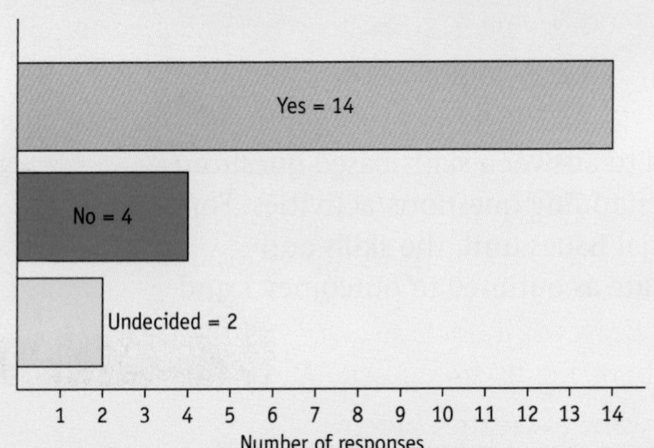

Source 2 – Interview with a focus group

Using my mobile phone, I will record a discussion session with a focus group of 3 of my classmates. I will ask the following question:

Why do people in East Dunbartonshire (where we live) live longer than people in Glasgow?

I will then type up a transcript of the discussion to display on my poster and I will highlight any arguments which agree or disagree with my hypothesis.

My transcript may look like this:

Me: Do you think that it is poverty or lifestyle choices that explain why people in East Dunbartonshire live longer than people in Glasgow?

(Life expectancy for a man in East Dunbartonshire is 80, and in Glasgow it is 72.)

Person 1: I think that poverty is the main reason as Glasgow has a greater number of unemployed people living on low incomes and in poor housing.

Person 2: I disagree, I think that lifestyle is more important – too many people in Glasgow have bad diets and do not exercise enough.

Person 3: But many people living on a low income cannot afford to buy healthy food or have a subscription to a health club.

Person 2: That's true, but I still think that people living on a low income could smoke and drink less.

Source 3 – Secondary sources

In this section of my poster I will include a newspaper article on the topic that I have found and also evidence from the Register General for Scotland website. I will make sure to acknowledge the sources of these pieces of information.

Source 4 – My own knowledge

The final source section of my poster will be based on my own knowledge of the topic. I will organise this into arguments which agree or disagree with my hypothesis.

Research methods: For each source I will consider the relevance, the accuracy and whether it could contain bias.

Conclusion: At the bottom of my poster I will present my conclusion, which will consider whether my hypothesis of *Poverty is the main cause of health inequalities in Scotland* has been proved or disproved.

National 4 Social Issues in the United Kingdom

Assessment items

At National 4 you will be expected to answer a skills-based question/activity and knowledge and understanding questions/activities. For the internal assessment of this social issues unit, the skills and knowledge which will be assessed are as outlined in outcomes 1 and 2 below.

Outcome 1

- Ability to use a limited range of sources of information to make and justify decisions about social issues in Scotland in the United Kingdom, focusing on either social inequality or crime and the law.

Outcome 2

N4
- Straightforward description and brief explanations demonstrating knowledge and understanding of social issues in the United Kingdom, focusing on either social inequality or crime and the law.

Assessment evidence

Evidence for successful completion of both outcomes can be based on a range of activities:

- responses to questions
- a presentation
- information posters, or
- participation in group tasks.

The examples that follow are based on written responses.

National 4 Social Issues in the UK: Social Inequality

Skills Question

Study the information below, then answer the question that follows.

Fact File: Mrs Elliott

- Mrs Elliott is worried about someone breaking into her house.
- Mrs Elliott is becoming frail and now uses a walking stick.
- Mrs Elliott likes being independent.
- Mrs Elliott enjoys the company of others and having a chat with her neighbours.
- Mrs Elliott now finds it difficult to see when it is the dark.

N4

Option 1 Move into sheltered housing

- An alarm system has been installed in every room in the flat and there is a 24-hour warden service.
- Mrs Elliott would have her own flat, which would be especially designed to meet her needs.
- The sheltered housing complex has a communal lounge where residents can meet and has a range of social events.

Option 2 Remain in her own home

- This is Mrs Elliott's preferred option and she can be quite determined.
- She will still have her independence with the local shop around the corner.
- She has lived in her present detached two-floor home for 30 years and knows all the neighbours.

You are the social worker for Mrs Elliott. You have to decide whether it would be better for her to move into a sheltered housing complex or to remain in her own home.

Using the information above, **state which option you would choose**. Either:

- It would be better for Mrs Elliott to move into a sheltered housing complex (Option 1), or
- It would be better for Mrs Elliott to remain in her present home (Option 2).

Give two reasons to support your answer.

In your answer you must link the option you choose to the information in the Fact File about Mrs Elliott.

Your answer must be based entirely on the information above. **(4 marks)**

Knowledge and Understanding Question

The government has tried to improve the health of the Scottish people.

(a) Describe **two** ways that the government has tried to improve the health of the Scottish people. **(4 marks)**

Schools should only sell healthy foods.

(b) Give **two** reasons why schools should only sell healthy foods. **(4 marks)**

National 4 Social Issues in the UK: Crime and the Law

Skills Question

Study the information below, then answer the question that follows.

Fact File: Louise Watt

- Louise's parents have recently separated and her mum is finding it difficult to cope.
- Louise has not attended school for months and feels she will struggle if she returns.
- Louise says that her only friends are the group who hang about in the street.
- Louise's father is now aware of the problem and wants to be more involved in her life.
- Louise is 14 and has been taken home on three occasions by police because of her antisocial behaviour and under-age drinking.

N4

Option 1 Louise should be sent to a Children's Panel for a hearing

- Children's Panels are not there to punish but aim to help vulnerable children and try to resolve their problems.
- A school Guidance teacher will attend the Panel and provide Louise with the support and confidence she needs to return to school.
- Children's Panels will listen to Louise in a relaxed environment.

Option 2 Louise should be given an official police warning

- The police are keen to tackle antisocial behaviour and under-age drinking directly with the individuals involved.
- Parents of young people under the age of 16 must attend a formal meeting at the police station.
- An official police warning might give Louise the fright she needs to start behaving in a responsible way, or it might make her even more resentful.

You are a Reporter to a Children's Panel. You have to decide whether to recommend that Louise Watt's case should be sent to the Children's Panel or whether she should be given an official police warning.

Using the information above, **state which option you would choose**. Either:

- Louise should be sent to a Children's Panel for a hearing (Option 1), or
- Louise should be given an official police warning (Option 2).

Give **two** reasons to support your choice.

In your answer, you must link the option you choose to the information in the Fact File on Louise Watt.

Your answer must be based only on the information above. **(4 marks)**

Outcome 2: Knowledge and Understanding Question

The Scottish legal system has different types of adult courts.

(a) Describe **two** types of adult courts in Scotland. **(4 marks)**

The 'not proven' verdict in Scottish court cases is a controversial issue.

(b) Give **two** reasons why some people criticise the 'not proven' verdict. **(4 marks)**

National 4 Added Value Unit

The assignment

The Added Value unit will be internally marked by your teacher. The SQA's unit specification document states that in order to pass the assignment you must research and use information relating to a Modern Studies topic or issue by:

- **Choosing, with support, an appropriate Modern Studies topic or issue.** You should choose an issue that you are interested in from any part of the course. Below are some examples from the social issues unit:
  - Poverty is the main cause of health inequalities in Scotland.
  - Scotland is the sick man of Europe.
  - The glass ceiling still exists in the United Kingdom.
  - Poverty was the main cause of the 2011 English riots.
  - Children's Panels are a soft option.
  - The 'not-proven' verdict does not deliver justice.
- **Collecting relevant evidence** from at least two different sources. The section on research methods (see pages 104–105) provides useful information on the types of sources that can be used.
- **Organising and using information** collected to address a topic or issue. You should use your skills to decide if the information is balanced or biased and based on fact rather than opinion.
- **Using the knowledge and understanding** you now have to describe and explain the key learning points you wish to make.
- **Applying your Modern Studies skills** in detecting bias or exaggeration, making decisions and drawing conclusions.
- **Presenting your findings and conclusion** on the issue you have chosen. You can present your findings in a variety of ways: as a written piece of research, or a poster, or a talk followed by questions, or you can use digital media such as a blog or journal.

National 4 Added Value Checklist

Name			
Title			
Unit(s)	Democracy in Scotland and the United Kingdom	Social Issues in the United Kingdom	International Issues
Relevant sources of information			
Number and type			
Evidence evaluated			
Skills used			
Detecting bias and exaggeration			
Making decisions			
Drawing conclusions			
Type of presentation			
Written report			
PowerPoint			
Wall display/Other			
Conclusion/Findings			
Based on evidence			
Evidence of individual work (if task is a group/paired activity)			

N4

National 5 Social Issues in the UK

Assessment items

At National 5 you will be expected to answer a skills-based question/ activity and knowledge and understanding questions/activities. For the internal assessment of this social issues unit, the skills and knowledge which will be assessed are as outlined in outcomes 1 and 2 below.

Outcome 1

- Ability to use a range of sources of information to make and justify a decision about social issues in the United Kingdom, focusing on either social inequality or crime and the law.

Outcome 2

- Detailed description and explanations demonstrating knowledge and understanding of social issues in the United Kingdom, focusing on either social inequality or crime and the law.

N5

Assessment evidence

Evidence for successful completion of both outcomes can be based on a range of activities:

- responses to questions
- a presentation
- information posters, or
- participation in group tasks.

The examples that follow are based on written responses.

National 5 Social Issues in the UK: Social Inequality

Skills Question

Study sources 1–3 and the options below, and then answer the question that follows.

Option 1

Continue with the Educational Maintenance Allowance (EMA).

Option 2

Do not continue with the Educational Maintenance Allowance (EMA).

N5

Source 1

Selected facts and viewpoints

If you are 16–19 years old in a school or college and come from a low-income family you can apply for the Educational Maintenance Allowance (EMA). This allowance is means tested and pays you £30 per week. To qualify for this allowance, the family income must be below £20,345 for a family with one child and £22,403 for a family with two or more children. The allowance was set up to encourage young people from poor backgrounds to stay in education and training once they reach the age of 16.

- EMA has been scrapped in England by the Conservative–Liberal Democrat Coalition Government. It argued that the significant cuts in public spending meant that hard decisions have to be made.
- The Scottish Government has cut funding by 20% and ended the £10 and £20 payment.
- Massive cuts are being made to the welfare budget, and education must take its share of reduced spending.
- Young people with poorer S4 results but who stay on at school beyond 16 do better in terms of employment in their late teens and early twenties.
- Since 2008, with the economic crisis, youth employment in Scotland has risen by 7,000.
- Almost 30% of young people who receive EMA live in Scotland's 15% most deprived areas.
- EMA is an investment in the future. It offers an escape from low-paid employment or a future of unemployment.

Source 2

Results of opinion poll survey

Should the Educational Maintenance Allowance (EMA) be scrapped?

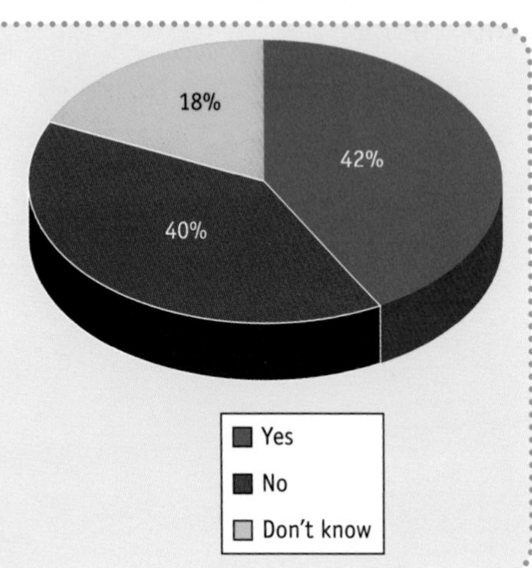

N5

Source 3

Educational Maintenance Allowance (EMA) should continue. Students use the money to cover the costs of books and other equipment for the course. In schools it enables students to attend conferences or activities outside the school without placing a burden on home finances. It has been a great success and has encouraged students to aim for better qualifications. In the past many would have left school at 16 without any qualifications and ended up without an apprenticeship or employment. EMA allows these youngsters to raise their goals and aspirations. This will help to reduce youth crime and create a more skilled workforce. A young person on a BBC website summed up the importance of EMA: 'I need EMA, otherwise I will have no education, in other words no future.' *(Lisa Sheerin)*

Educational Maintenance Allowance (EMA) should not continue. It can favour students whose parents are self-employed and who use an accountant to reduce their taxable income. So it is unfair as other students who just miss the payment receive nothing. So for some young people the allowance can be saved up to go on a holiday at the end of the school year. This is a waste of taxpayers' money. We are cutting back on spending in health and education and this money should be spent on more essential services. Further cuts will be made to the welfare budget in the period 2013–15 and we need to protect our poor pensioners and other vulnerable groups and stop spending it on the wasteful EMA. *(John King)*

You are an adviser to the Scottish Government. You have been asked to recommend whether or not to continue with Education Maintenance Allowance (EMA).

You must decide which option to recommend to the Scottish Government. Either:

- To continue with the Educational Maintenance Allowance (EMA) (Option 1), or
- Not to continue with the Educational Maintenance Allowance (EMA) (Option 2).

Using sources 1, 2 and 3, which option would you choose?

Give reasons to **support** your choice.

Explain why you did not make the other choice.

Your answer must be based on all three sources. **(10 marks)**

Knowledge and Understanding Question

Gender inequalities still exist in the United Kingdom workforce.

(a) Describe, **in detail, two** ways in which gender inequalities exist in the workforce. **(4 marks)**

Poor health is still suffered by many people in the United Kingdom.

(b) Explain, **in detail**, the reasons why some people experience poorer health than others. **(6 marks)**

National 5 Skills Question: Social Issues in the UK: Crime and the Law

Skills Question

Study sources 1–3 below, and then answer the question that follows.

Option 1
The DNA database should contain only profiles of convicted criminals.

Option 2
The DNA database should contain profiles of the whole population.

Source 1

Selected facts and viewpoints

The UK National DNA database was set up in 1995 and responsibility in Scotland lies with the Police Forensic Science Lab. The UK is a world leader in this field and has the largest DNA database in the world. In Scotland DNA evidence is retained for a limited time for those convicted of a crime. In England it also includes those charged with a crime.

Current viewpoints include:

- It would be the ultimate step on the road to a 'Big Brother' state: Britain would become 'a nation of suspects'.
- Those who do nothing wrong have nothing to fear and should be reassured.
- The current system is selective and inefficient. A DNA database covering the whole population and every visitor to the UK would save massive amounts of police time and help clear up crimes faster.
- Financial savings would be made if everyone's DNA was taken once.
- DNA samples increase the likelihood of accurate verdicts in court cases.
- It would be very expensive and time-consuming to set up.
- Whatever the benefits of universal DNA sampling, it would be a step too far to enter every baby on a DNA database at birth.

Source 2

Results of opinion poll survey

Should all citizens of the United Kingdom be required to give a sample of DNA?

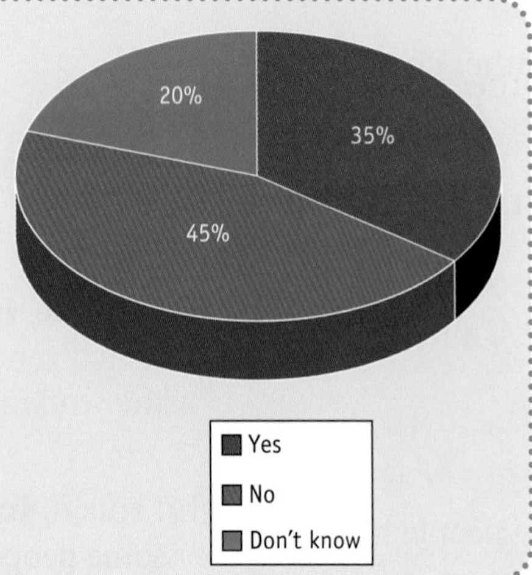

Source 3

A national database holding a record of the DNA of every man, woman and child in the country may seem extreme. However, such a database would enable police forces to put behind bars the serious offenders who carry out violent assault and commit murder. In a recent murder case the accused would have been arrested within 24 hours of the death of his young victim had a national DNA database existed. DNA from the suspect was critical to the jury finding him guilty of the murder, but the police only managed to get his DNA by chance, after he was arrested for his part in a scuffle in a pub. DNA samples increase the likelihood of accurate verdicts in court cases. They reduce the chances of convicting the innocent or freeing the guilty. Innocent citizens have nothing to fear from registering, any more than we should fear giving our fingerprints or worry that the Inland Revenue holds details on where we work and how much we earn.

Civil Liberties Spokesperson

The UK already has the highest number of citizens whose DNA records are held by the state. In the USA one in every 100 persons has their DNA profiles recorded; in contrast in the UK it is five in every 100. Few of us can have much confidence that governments would treat the information held on a national DNA database in accordance with the highest standards of confidentiality and integrity that would be required to keep the inevitable, inadvertent, abuses to a minimum level. Blunders and mistakes by officials charged with keeping the records would lead to an unacceptable level of intrusion in the lives of Britain's citizens. The European Court of Human Rights has stated that no innocent citizen should have their DNA recorded by the state.

Police Spokesperson

N5 You are an adviser to the Scottish Government. You have been asked to recommend whether the DNA database should keep only the profiles of criminals or whether it should contain profiles of the whole population.

You must decide which option to recommend to the Scottish Government. Either:

- It should retain only the DNA profiles of criminals (Option 1), or
- It should contain DNA profiles of the whole population (Option 2).

Using sources 1, 2 and 3, which option would you choose?

Give reasons to **support** your choice.

Explain why you did not make the other choice.

Your answer must be based on all three sources. **(8 marks)**

Knowledge and Understanding Question

The Children's Panel tries to resolve the problems faced by young people.

(a) Describe, **in detail**, ways in which the Children's Panel tries to resolve the problems faced by young people. **(4 marks)**

Some areas of Scotland have higher crime rates than others.

(b) Explain, **in detail**, the reasons why some areas of Scotland have higher crime than others. **(6 marks)**

National 5 Course Assessment

Added Value is assessed in the course assessment and is made up of two components:

- a question paper with activities from each of the three units
- National 5 assignment.

Course Assessment Structure

Component 1 – Question paper

The question paper is worth a total of 60 marks, with 20 marks for each unit of the course. Overall, 26 marks are for skills and 34 marks are for knowledge and understanding. The duration of the exam is 1 hour and 30 minutes.

Component 2 – Assignment

The assignment is worth a total of 20 marks. Of these, 14 marks are for skills and 6 marks are for knowledge and understanding.

Total marks available 80 marks

N5

To gain the course award all units and course assessment must be passed. The marks you achieve in the question paper and assignment are added together and an overall mark will indicate a pass or fail. From this, your course award will then be graded.

National 5 Assignment

The National 5 assignment is a personal research activity which must include at least two methods of collecting information with comment on the effectiveness of the methods used. The information collected should display knowledge and understanding of the topic or issue chosen. The results of your research will be written up under controlled assessment conditions. As previously mentioned, 20 marks are given to the assignment.

Preparation for the assignment

1 Research question

You should choose an appropriate topic or issue, for example, *Lifestyle choice is the main cause of health inequalities in Scotland* (see page 111 for examples of other topics). You may choose an issue from any of the three individual units or you may choose a topic that integrates two units of the course, for example *Election systems in Scotland and South Africa have similarities and differences*. The best practice is to present the research question in the form of a hypothesis with clear aim.

2 Research methods

As part of your assignment, you must gather relevant evidence to support your hypothesis using at least two methods of collecting information. There is a range of methods you could use, including field work, referencing books or the Internet. You are expected to evaluate the strengths and weaknesses of each research method you use and to analyse your findings. Remember that two methods are the minimum you are required to use and you might wish to widen your range to more than two.

3 Research findings

This is the section which will display your detailed knowledge and understanding in describing and explaining issues relevant to your hypothesis, including the identification of a variety of viewpoints. Here you must also evaluate the evidence you have gathered and describe what it shows.

4 Research conclusions

Once you have successfully analysed and explained the information you have gathered, you should make conclusions based on your research. Your conclusions must be relevant to your research issue and link back to your original hypothesis. Try to avoid simply repeating the findings you have previously given.